2

STUDY GUIDE

Medicine in Britain, c1250–present and the British Sector of the Western Front, 1914–18: Injuries, Treatment and the Trenches

Edexcel - GCSE

Published by Clever Lili Limited.

contact@cleverlili.com

First published 2020

ISBN 978-1-913887-01-8

Copyright notice

All rights reserved. No part of this publication may be reproduced in any form or by any means (including photocopying or storing it in any medium by electronic means and whether or not transiently or incidentally to some other use of this publication) with the written permission of the copyright owner. Applications for the copyright owner's written permission should be addressed to the publisher.

Clever Lili has made every effort to contact copyright holders for permission for the use of copyright material. We will be happy, upon notification, to rectify any errors or omissions and include any appropriate rectifications in future editions.

Cover by: Robert Riggs/Everett Collection on Shutterstock

Icons by: flaticon and freepik

Contributors: Hayleigh Snow, Rebecca Lawrence, Emily Bishop, Lynn Harkin, Marcus Pailing, Shahan Abu Shumel Haydar, Jen Mellors

Edited by Paul Connolly and Rebecca Parsley

Design by Evgeni Veskov and Will Fox

All rights reserved

DISCOVER MORE OF OUR GCSE HISTORY STUDY GUIDES
GCSEHistory.com and Clever Lili

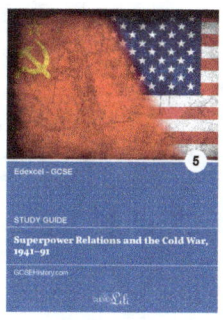
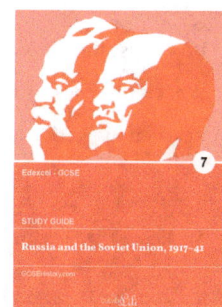

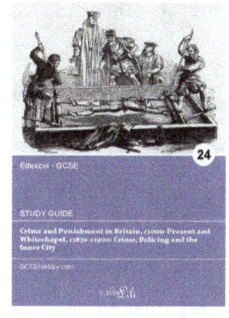

THE GUIDES ARE EVEN BETTER WITH OUR GCSE/IGCSE HISTORY WEBSITE APP AND MOBILE APP

GCSE History is a text and voice web and mobile app that allows you to easily revise for your GCSE/IGCSE exams wherever you are - it's like having your own personal GCSE history tutor. Whether you're at home or on the bus, GCSE History provides you with thousands of convenient bite-sized facts to help you pass your exams with flying colours. We cover all topics - with more than 120,000 questions - across the Edexcel, AQA and CIE exam boards.

Contents

How to use this book ... 6
What is this book about? ... 7
Revision suggestions ... 9

Timelines
Medicine Through Time, c1250 - Present Day ... 13

Medicine in Medieval England, c1250-c1500
Beliefs in the Causes of Disease ... 18
Superstitious Beliefs ... 18
Rational Beliefs ... 19
The Four Humours ... 19
Hippocrates ... 20
Galen ... 21
Treatments ... 22
Prevention ... 23
Hospitals ... 24
Physicians ... 24
Apothecaries ... 25
Medieval Surgery ... 26
Barber Surgeons ... 26
Leprosy ... 27
Black Death ... 28
Medicine - Change & Continuity ... 29

Medicine in Renaissance England, c1500-c1700
Renaissance ... 30
Printing Press ... 31
Johannes Gutenberg ... 32
Treatments ... 32
Prevention ... 33
Royal Society ... 33
Andreas Vesalius ... 34
William Harvey ... 35
Thomas Sydenham ... 36
Hospitals - Change & Continuity ... 37
Pest Houses ... 38
Great Plague ... 38
Great Plague & Black Death Compared ... 39

Medicine in Industrial Britain, c1700-c1900
Laissez-Faire ... 40
Belief in Causes of Disease - Change & Continuity ... 40
Inoculation ... 41
Edward Jenner and Vaccination ... 42

Louis Pasteur's Germ Theory ... 43
Robert Koch ... 45
C18th Hospitals - Change & Continuity ... 45
Florence Nightingale ... 46
Surgery in the C19th ... 48
Robert Liston ... 49
James Blundell ... 49
Anaesthetics ... 49
Nitrous Oxide ... 50
Humphry Davy ... 50
Ether ... 51
Chloroform ... 51
Hannah Greener ... 52
Cocaine ... 53
James Simpson ... 53
Antiseptics ... 53
Carbolic Acid ... 53
Joseph Lister ... 54
Aseptic Surgery ... 55
Industrialisation ... 55
Disease in Industrial Cities ... 56
Edwin Chadwick ... 57
First Public Health Act ... 58
Sanitary Act ... 58
Cholera ... 59
John Snow ... 60
The Great Stink ... 60
Joseph Bazalgette ... 61
Second Public Health Act ... 62

Medicine in Modern Britain, c1900-the Present Day
Blood Groups ... 62
Karl Landsteiner ... 63
Magic Bullets ... 64
Prontosil ... 65
Paul Ehrlich ... 65
Sahachiro Hata ... 66
Gerhard Domagk ... 66
Alexander Fleming ... 66
Penicillin and Antibiotics ... 67
Howard Florey ... 68
Ernst Chain ... 69
Radiation ... 69
Marie Curie ... 69

X-Rays	70
Wilhelm Roentgen	70
Genetic Understanding	71
The Human Genome Project	71
James Watson	72
Francis Crick	72
Rosalind Franklin	72
Maurice Wilkins	73
New Technology in the 20th Century	73
Alternative Medicine	74
Prevention	75
Diphtheria	76
Emil von Behring	76
Polio	77
Jonas Salk	77
Lung Cancer	77
Welfare State	79
William Beveridge	80
Aneurin Bevan	80
NHS	81

The British Sector of the Western Front, 1914-1918: Injuries, Treatments and the Trenches

The First World War Context	82
Ypres	83
First Battle of Ypres	84
Hill 60	84
Second Battle of Ypres	85
Battle of the Somme	85
Battle of Arras	86
The Battle of Passchendaele	87
Battle of Cambrai	87
Trench System	88
New Weapons	89
Mud	89
Trench Illnesses	90
Shell Shock	90
Trench Foot	91
Trench Fever	92
Dysentery	92
Gangrene	93
The Use of Gas	93
Treatments	94
Thomas Splint	95
Carrel-Dakin Method	95
RAMC	95

Regimental Aid Posts	96
Advanced Dressing Stations	96
Main Dressing Stations	97
Casualty Clearing Stations	97
Base Hospitals	98
Nursing	98
FANY	99
VAD	99
Transport	100
Plastic Surgery	101
Harold Gillies	101
Brain Surgery	102
Harvey Cushing	102
Blood Transfusions	103
Lawrence Bruce Robertson	104
Richard Weil	104
Richard Lewisohn	104
Francis Rous	104
James Turner	105
X-rays	105
Glossary	106
Index	110

HOW TO USE THIS BOOK

In this study guide, you will see a series of icons, highlighted words and page references. The key below will help you quickly establish what these mean and where to go for more information.

Icons

 WHAT questions cover the key events and themes.

 WHO questions cover the key people involved.

 WHEN questions cover the timings of key events.

 WHERE questions cover the locations of key moments.

 WHY questions cover the reasons behind key events.

 HOW questions take a closer look at the way in which events, situations and trends occur.

 IMPORTANCE questions take a closer look at the significance of events, situations, and recurrent trends and themes.

 DECISIONS questions take a closer look at choices made at events and situations during this era.

Highlighted words

Abdicate - occasionally, you will see certain words highlighted within an answer. This means that, if you need it, you'll find an explanation of the word or phrase in the glossary which starts on **page 106**.

Page references

Tudor *(p.7)* - occasionally, a certain subject within an answer is covered in more depth on a different page. If you'd like to learn more about it, you can go directly to the page indicated.

WHAT IS THIS BOOK ABOUT?

Medicine through time, c1250 - present, is a thematic study that looks at the change and continuity of medicine through British history. You will study the main people, events and developments, as well as the significant features of the different ages, from medieval to modern times. In studying the Western Front during the First World War, you will investigate a historic environment that was significant to the development of medicine.

Purpose
In studying this course you will be able to view the process of change and continuity across time and make comparisons between different ages. You will assess how different themes played a part to instigate or hold back changes. Through the study of the Western Front, you will develop an understanding of the use of sources in a historical enquiry.

Topics
Within each of the time periods the course looks at specific topics. These are:
- Causes of disease.
- Treatments for diseases.
- Prevention of diseases.
- Who treated people.
- Hospitals and their use.
- Individuals and their impact.

Key Themes
Throughout the course you can see that some of these themes have an impact on the changes and continuities that occur. They can either hinder or help change to occur. These themes are:
- Scientific discoveries.
- Technology and communication.
- People's attitudes and beliefs, including religion.
- Government action or inaction.
- Individuals and their impact.
- War and the need for change.

Key timeperiods
The medicine through time course is split into time periods. Across which you will need to discuss the changes and continuities that occur. These time periods are:
- Medicine in Medieval England, c1250 - c1500.
- Medicine in Renaissance England, c1500 - c1700.
- Medicine in Industrial Britain, c1700 - c1900.
- Medicine in Modern Britain, c1900 - present day.
- The British sector of the Western Front, 1914-1918: injuries, treatments and the trenches.

Assessment
Medicine through time, c1250 - present, is assessed by Paper 1, and is worth 30% of your overall grade. The paper is split into two sections.
- Section A focuses on the historical environment of the Western Front. This consists of a knowledge-based question and a two-part question based on two historical sources.
- Section B contains three questions that assess your knowledge and understanding of the thematic part of the course.

Section A
Section A contains Question 1, a knowledge-based question, and Question 2, a two-part question based on two sources.
- Question 1 is worth 4 marks. It will ask you describe two features of the Western Front.
- Question 2(a) is worth 8 marks. It will ask you about the usefulness of two sources in reference to a particular historical enquiry. You will be required to refer to both sources and your own knowledge in your answer.

WHAT IS THIS BOOK ABOUT?

- Question 2(b) is worth 4 marks. It will ask you how you would follow up on one of the sources to continue the particular historical enquiry. You will be required to choose a detail from the source to continue your study, to give a question that you could ask to find out more, the type of source that you could use for your investigation and to explain how that would help your enquiry.

Section B

Section B contains Question 3, an explanation of similarities between different periods and Question 4, an explanation of change or consequence. You will have a choice of one between Questions 5 and 6, which will give you a historical interpretation to support and challenge.

- Question 3 is worth 4 marks. It will ask you to compare an issue across two different periods of time, either through their similarities or differences.
- Question 4 is worth 12 marks. It will ask you 'why' and you need to give three explained reasons linking to the topic they ask about. They will give you two bullet points that you can use but you must have a point of your own to show use of your own knowledge.
- Question 5 and 6 are both worth 16 marks plus 4 marks for spelling, punctuation and grammar. You pick ONE to answer with three explained reasons, which need to include an agree and disagree point. They will give you two bullet points that you can use but you must have a point of your own to show key own knowledge. You must have a conclusion too.

REVISION SUGGESTIONS

Revision! A dreaded word. Everyone knows it's coming, everyone knows how much it helps with your exam performance, and everyone struggles to get started! We know you want to do the best you can in your GCSEs, but schools aren't always clear on the best way to revise. This can leave students wondering:

- ✓ How should I plan my revision time?
- ✓ How can I beat procrastination?
- ✓ What methods should I use? Flash cards? Re-reading my notes? Highlighting?

Luckily, you no longer need to guess at the answers. Education researchers have looked at all the available revision studies, and the jury is in. They've come up with some key pointers on the best ways to revise, as well as some thoughts on popular revision methods that aren't so helpful. The next few pages will help you understand what we know about the best revision methods.

How can I beat procrastination?

This is an age-old question, and it applies to adults as well! Have a look at our top three tips below.

⊚ Reward yourself

When we think a task we have to do is going to be boring, hard or uncomfortable, we often put if off and do something more 'fun' instead. But we often don't really enjoy the 'fun' activity because we feel guilty about avoiding what we should be doing. Instead, get your work done and promise yourself a reward after you complete it. Whatever treat you choose will seem all the sweeter, and you'll feel proud for doing something you found difficult. Just do it!

⊚ Just do it!

We tend to procrastinate when we think the task we have to do is going to be difficult or dull. The funny thing is, the most uncomfortable part is usually making ourselves sit down and start it in the first place. Once you begin, it's usually not nearly as bad as you anticipated.

⊚ Pomodoro technique

The pomodoro technique helps you trick your brain by telling it you only have to focus for a short time. Set a timer for 20 minutes and focus that whole period on your revision. Turn off your phone, clear your desk, and work. At the end of the 20 minutes, you get to take a break for five. Then, do another 20 minutes. You'll usually find your rhythm and it becomes easier to carry on because it's only for a short, defined chunk of time.

Spaced practice

We tend to arrange our revision into big blocks. For example, you might tell yourself: "This week I'll do all my revision for the Cold War, then next week I'll do the Medicine Through Time unit."

REVISION SUGGESTIONS

This is called **massed practice**, because all revision for a single topic is done as one big mass.

But there's a better way! Try **spaced practice** instead. Instead of putting all revision sessions for one topic into a single block, space them out. See the example below for how it works.

This means planning ahead, rather than leaving revision to the last minute - but the evidence strongly suggests it's worth it. You'll remember much more from your revision if you use **spaced practice** rather than organising it into big blocks. Whichever method you choose, though, remember to reward yourself with breaks.

Spaced practice (more effective):

week 1	week 2	week 3	week 4
Topic 1	Topic 1	Topic 1	Topic 1
Topic 2	Topic 2	Topic 2	Topic 2
Topic 3	Topic 3	Topic 3	Topic 3
Topic 4	Topic 4	Topic 4	Topic 4

Massed practice (less effective)

week 1	week 2	week 3	week 4
Topic 1	Topic 2	Topic 3	Topic 4

REVISION SUGGESTIONS

What methods should I use to revise?

Self-testing/flash cards

Self explanation/mind-mapping

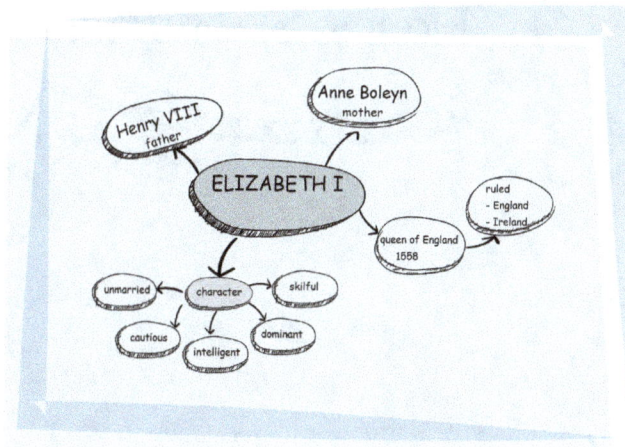

The research shows a clear winner for revision methods - **self-testing**. A good way to do this is with <mark>flash cards.</mark> Flash cards are really useful for helping you recall short – but important – pieces of information, like names and dates.

Side A - question   Side B - answer

Write questions on one side of the cards, and the answers on the back. This makes answering the questions and then testing yourself easy. Put all the cards you get right in a pile to one side, and only repeat the test with the ones you got wrong - this will force you to work on your weaker areas.

pile with right answers

pile with wrong answers

As this book has a quiz question structure itself, you can use it for this technique.

Another good revision method is **self-explanation**. This is where you explain how and why one piece of information from your course linked with another piece.

This can be done with <mark>mind-maps,</mark> where you draw the links and then write explanations for how they connect. For example, President Truman is connected with anti-communism because of the Truman Doctrine.

Get our free app at GCSEHistory.com

REVISION SUGGESTIONS

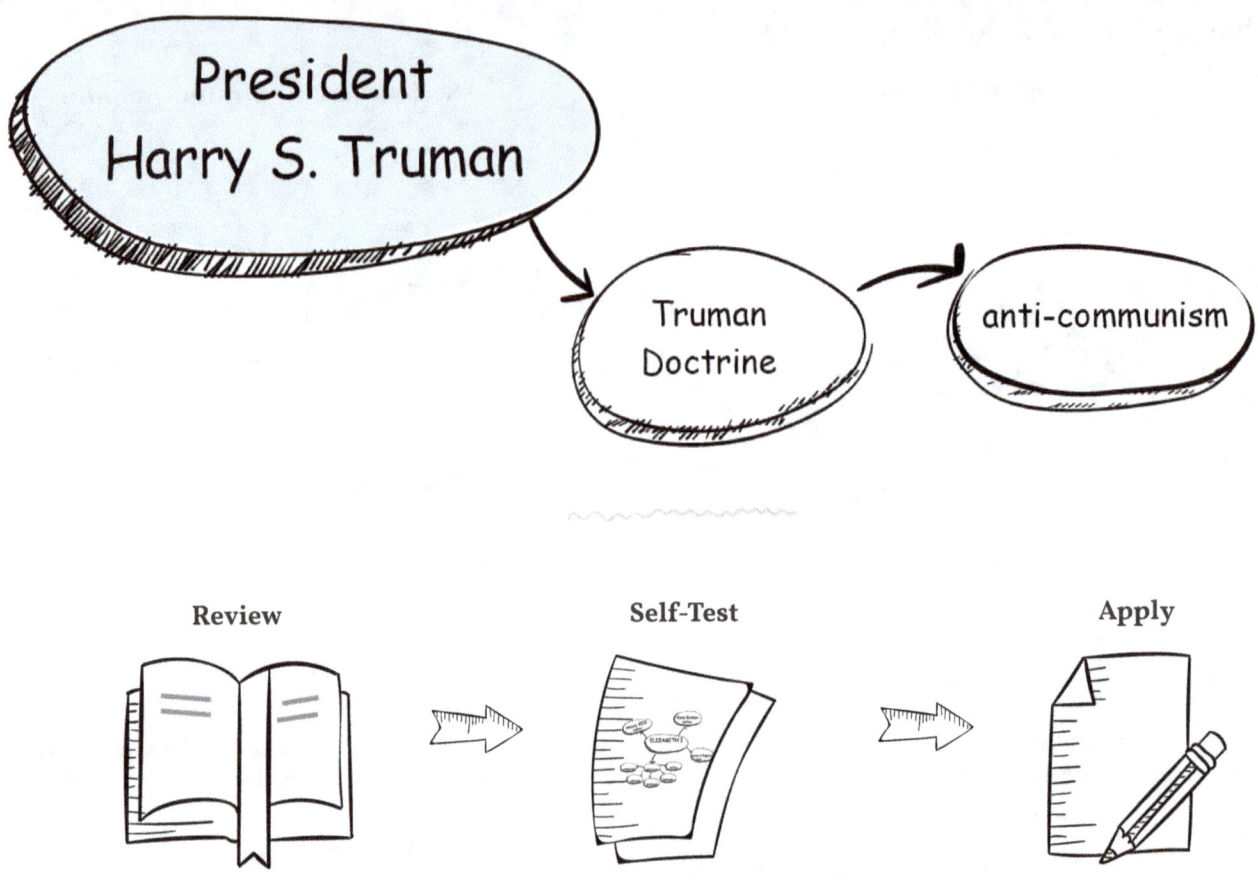

Start by highlighting or re-reading to create your flashcards for self-testing.

Test yourself with flash cards. Make mind maps to explain the concepts.

Apply your knowledge on practice exam questions.

 Which revision techniques should I be cautious about?

Highlighting and **re-reading** are not necessarily bad strategies - but the research does say they're less effective than flash cards and mind-maps.

If you do use these methods, make sure they are **the first step to creating flash cards**. Really engage with the material as you go, rather than switching to autopilot.

MEDICINE THROUGH TIME, C1250 - PRESENT DAY

TIMELINE

- **1348** — Black Death arrived in England (p.28)
- **1440** — Invention of the printing press (p.31)
- **1536** — Henry VIII began the dissolution of monasteries in England (p.37)
- **1537** — Vesalius's first publication 'Six Anatomical Tables' (p.34)
- **1628** — Harvey published 'An Anatomical Account of the Motion of the Heart and Blood in Animals' (p.35)
- **1664** — The Great Plague (p.38)
- **1665** — Royal Society published its first scientific journal 'Philosophical Transactions' (p.33)
- **1795** — Davy discovered that nitrous oxide numbs pain (p.50)
- **1796** — Harvey proved the circulation of the blood
- **1798** — Jenner published his findings 'An Enquiry into the Causes and Effects of the Variolae Vaccinae' (p.42)
- **1818** — Blundell experimented with blood transfusions (p.63)
- **1831** — First cholera outbreak in Britain (p.59)
- **1842** — Ether used in dentistry for the first time (p.51)
- **1846** — Liston successfully anaesthetised a patient for a leg amputation (p.49)
- **1842** — Chadwick published his 'Report on the Sanitary Conditions of the Labouring Classes' (p.57)
- **1847** — Simpson discovered the use of chloroform as an anaesthetic (p.53)
- **1848** — The First Public Health Act (p.58)
- **1852** — Smallpox vaccination became compulsory
- **1853** — Chloroform used successfully to help Queen Victoria give birth to her 8th child (p.51)
- **1854** — Britain at war with Russia in the Crimea
- **1854** — The link between cholera and water was discovered (p.60)

MEDICINE THROUGH TIME, C1250 - PRESENT DAY

1858 — The Great Stink (p.60)

1860 — The Nightingale School for Nurses was opened at St Thomas' Hospital (p.46)

1861 — Pasteur published his germ theory (p.43)

1865 — Lister used carbolic acid-soaked dressings for the first time (p.54)
1865 - 1,300 miles of sewer were built in London (p.61)

1866 — The Sanitary Act (p.58)
1866 - Last cholera outbreak in Britain (p.59)

1872 — Enforcement of the compulsory smallpox vaccination

1875 — The Second Public Health Act (p.62)

1879 — Pasteur created a vaccine for chicken cholera (p.43)

1883 — Koch discovered the microbes responsible for cholera and diptheria (p.45)

1890 — von Behring created a vaccine for tetanus and diphtheria (p.76)

1895 — Roentgen developed the X-Ray machine (p.70)

1901 — Landsteiner discovered blood groups A, B and O (p.63)

1909 — The First Magic Bullet, Salvarsan 606, was discovered (p.64)

1914 — First World War started (p.82)
October - The First Battle of Ypres (p.83)
October - First six FANYs arrived in France (p.99)
November - First ambulance train arrived in France (p.100)
April - Hill 60 (p.84)

1915 — Lewisohn discovered that adding sodium citrate to blood stops it clotting (p.103)
April - The Second Battle of Ypres (p.93)

1916 — Rous and Turner found that using citrate glucose in blood allows 4 weeks of storage (p.103)
July - The Battle of the Somme

1917 — *April* - The Battle of Arras (p.86)
July - The Third Battle of Ypres (p.83)

Quizzes, amazing exam preparation tools and more at GCSEHistory.com

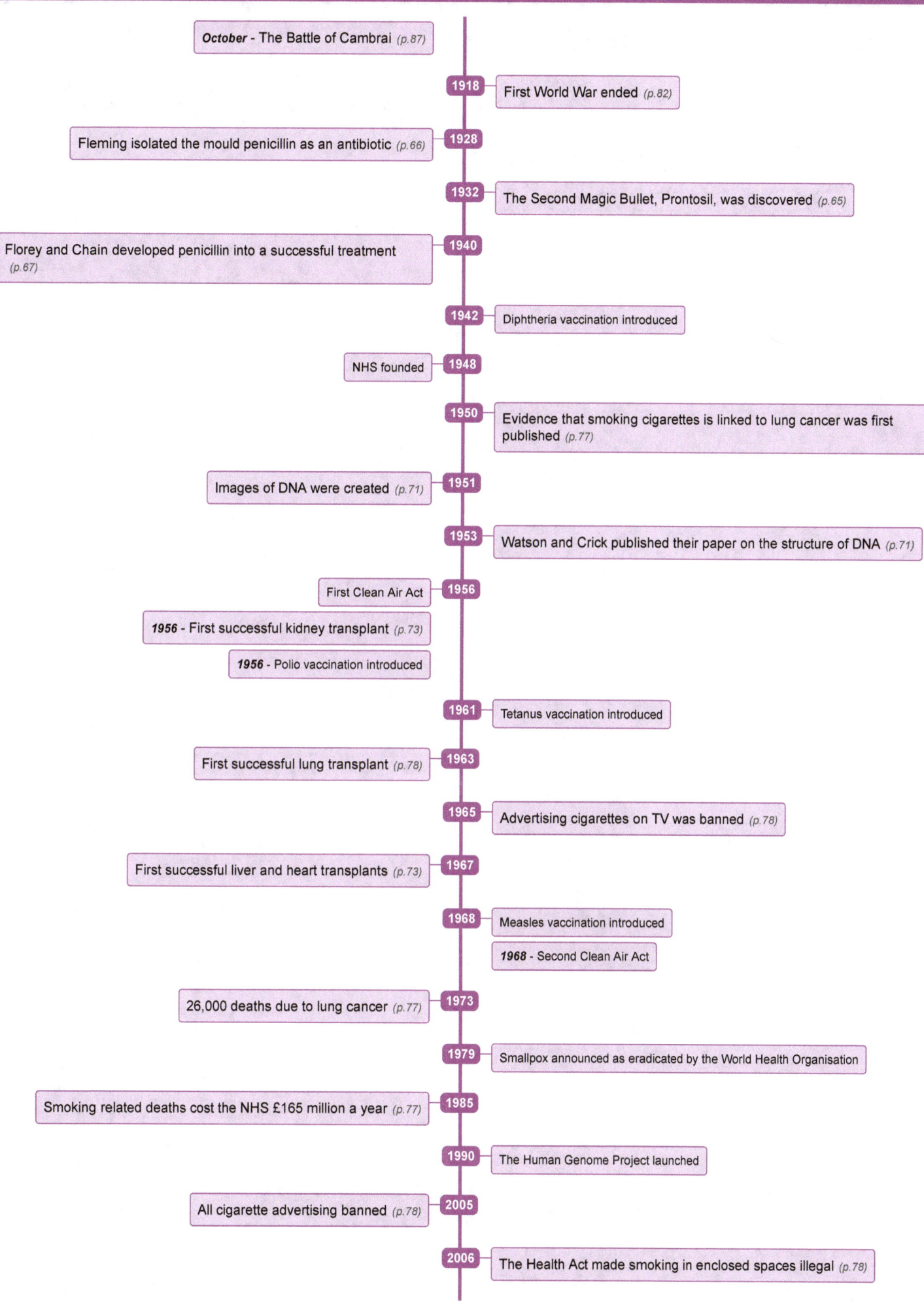

MEDICINE THROUGH TIME, C1250 - PRESENT DAY

2007 — Smoking banned in workplaces, and the legal age to buy tobacco raised to 18 (p.78)

2012 — Cigarettes no longer allowed to be on display in shops (p.78)

2015 — Change4Life campaign launched

2015 - Smoking in cars carrying children banned (p.78)

MEDICINE THROUGH TIME, C1250 - PRESENT DAY

BELIEFS IN THE CAUSES OF DISEASE
Rational and supernatural explanations

? What were medieval beliefs about disease?
The causes of disease were a mystery. People believed supernatural *(p.18)* causes could lead to illness.

SUPERSTITIOUS BELIEFS
Punishments, tests, evil, and astrology

? What supernatural explanations did people hold about health?
People in medieval England often relied on superstition when it came to health. They believed in supernatural explanations for health and disease.

What were the most common supernatural explanations of causes of disease in the medieval period?
There were 4 main supernatural elements believed to cause disease.
- ✓ Many believed that diseases were the will of God. The Catholic Church taught that, if someone committed a sin, God would punish them with sickness.
- ✓ People believed that illness was a test of faith.
- ✓ Some people believed that supernatural demons could inhabit people's bodies and cause illnesses.
- ✓ Witches were thought to be responsible for spreading diseases.
- ✓ Some people thought astrology was to blame - that the way the stars and planets were aligned could cause disease.

Why did people have supernatural explanations about the causes of disease?
Religion was a major force in medieval England, and the Catholic Church had a lot of influence over people's lives. There was also a lack of scientific knowledge. This led to people believing in supernatural reasons for disease and sickness.

What were the main supernatural beliefs for treatment of disease in medieval medicine?
There were three main treatments for diseases based on superstitious beliefs.
- ✓ Prayers were said to ask God's forgiveness. The rich could pay for prayers to be said on their behalf. Many people used flagellation (whipping themselves).
- ✓ People went on pilgrimages to important religious shrines or tombs.
- ✓ Physicians used horoscopes to treat patients. They would consider two dates: the patient's date of birth and the date their illness began. They would use this information to work out how to treat them.

DID YOU KNOW?

One superstitious belief about the Black Death of 1348 was that it was caused by an astrological conjunction (meeting) of Jupiter, Saturn and Mars.

RATIONAL BELIEFS
Miasmas and humoural imbalance

 Were there any rational explanations for why people got sick?

Not all ideas about the causes of disease were based on supernatural *(p.18)* beliefs. Some were based on rational explanations.

 What were the rational explanations for the causes of disease?

People believed two main rational explanations for the causes of disease.
- ✓ Miasma theory was the idea that bad air from dead bodies, rotting food, or other organic matter caused disease.
- ✓ Another idea was the illness was caused by an imbalance of the 'four humours' within the body - blood, yellow bile (choler), black bile and phlegm.

> **DID YOU KNOW?**
>
> Some people in 1348 believed that the Black Death had been caused by an earthquake in China, which had released miasma - bad air.

THE FOUR HUMOURS
Blood, choler, black bile and phlegm

What was the humours theory?

The Theory of the Four Humours stated that, to be healthy, a person needed to have balanced humours. People would get diseases if they had too much or too little of any humour.

 What were the humours according to the Theory of the Four Humours?

There were four humours.
- ✓ Choler, or yellow bile, was considered hot and dry, and related to summer and fire.
- ✓ Blood was hot and wet, and related to spring and air.
- ✓ Phlegm was cold and wet, and related to winter and water.
- ✓ Black bile was considered cold and dry, and was related to autumn and earth.

 How did doctors balance yellow bile according to the Theory of the Four Humours?

To balance yellow bile (choler), doctors would purge patients, by making them vomit or by changing their diet.

 How did doctors balance blood according to the Theory of the Four Humours?

Bloodletting was used to balance blood. This was most often done by barber surgeons or wise women.

 How did doctors balance phlegm according to the Theory of the Four Humours?

To balance phlegm, doctors recommended breathing steam or eating vegetables filled with water.

How did doctors balance black bile according to the Theory of the Four Humours?

Doctors gave their patients laxatives and suggested they eat more vegetables to balance black bile.

How did Galen of Pergamon add to the Theory of the Four Humours?

Galen *(p.21)* built on the Theory of Four Humours by adding the Theory of Opposites for treating an imbalance. For example, he taught that too much blood (a fever) could be cured by cool things, such as eating cucumber.

Why was the Theory of the Four Humours important?

There are three main reasons why the Theory of the Four Humours was important.

- ☑ It became the basis for how patients were treated for more than 1,400 years.
- ☑ It appeared to include all illnesses. Therefore, in order to apply the theory, physicians would deliberately manipulate what they observed to fit it.
- ☑ There was a lack of scientific knowledge at that time which stopped people challenging the theory or providing alternative treatments.

> **DID YOU KNOW?**
>
> **Each humour was believed to cause a different sort of mood.**
>
> People with too much blood were thought to be 'sanguine' - cheerful and energetic. Too much choler made them bossy and 'choleric'. Too much black bile made them 'melancholic' and sad, while too much phlegm made them 'phlegmatic' - calm and slow to react.

HIPPOCRATES

The original 'Father of Medicine'

Who was Hippocrates?

Hippocrates was an ancient Greek physician. He believed in observing a patient's symptoms, and treating them using natural treatments.

What were Hippocrates' ideas?

There are three main theories attributed to Hippocrates.

- ☑ Clinical observation, which says a doctor should examine and monitor a patient's symptoms to diagnose their illness. Treatments should be based on these observations.
- ☑ The Hippocratic Oath, which was taken by physicians. It was a promise to follow a set of ethical standards to treat their patients well and to cause no harm.
- ☑ The Theory of the Four Humours, which says that a person needed balanced humours in order to be healthy. People got diseases if they had too much or too little of any humour *(p.19)*.

> **DID YOU KNOW?**
>
> Hippocrates lived in the 5th century BCE.

GALEN

Building on the Theory of the Four Humours with the Theory of Opposites

Who was Claudius Galen?

Claudius Galen was an ancient Roman physician, surgeon and writer of Greek origin. He was the personal surgeon to the Roman Empire Marcus Aurelius, and wrote over 350 books.

What were Galen's scientific beliefs?

Galen believed in the Theory of the Four Humours and built on it by developing the Theory of Opposites. He supported clinical observation, and encouraged doctors to monitor a patient's pulse or take a urine sample to determine what was wrong.

Why did the Christian Church support Galen?

Galen said that the human body must have been designed because it fit together so well. This supported the Church's teachings that God created humans.

What were Galen's theories?

There were two main theories associated with Galen.

- ☑ Galen based his Theory of Opposites on the Theory of the Four Humours. He taught that illnesses could be cured by using treatments that opposed a patient's symptoms. For example, if there was an excess of blood - which was considered hot and wet, and could lead to illnesses such as a fever - then the treatment should be cold and dry.
- ☑ Galen supported the miasma theory, which was the belief that disease was caused by bad air.

What mistakes did Galen make?

Galen had carried out some dissections on animals, as human dissection was forbidden by the Church. This meant he made some mistakes.

- ☑ He believed that the jaw was made up of two bones.
- ☑ He did not understand about blood circulation, and thought that blood was made in the liver, then absorbed by the body, rather than being pumped around it.
- ☑ He said that men had one fewer pair of ribs than women.

Why were Galen's ideas supported for so long?

Galen's ideas were significant for 2 main reasons:

- ☑ Galen's ideas had the support of the Church. Its influence over peoples' beliefs ensured his ideas were followed as the foundation of medicine for 1,400 years.
- ☑ There were a lack of alternatives to his ideas and little opportunity to question them.

Why were Galen's books important?

Galen's books were important because many people could not read, so any doctor who had read them was considered very intelligent.

What made Galen hard to challenge?

There was a lack of scientific evidence to challenge what Galen taught, because the Church would not allow human dissection.

> **DID YOU KNOW?**
> Over the course of his career, Galen was also a physician for gladiator schools.

TREATMENTS
Prayer and phlebotomy

What was medieval treatment like?
Medieval treatment *(p.29)* was very limited as it was mostly based on the supposed superstitious and religious causes of disease. It was also sometimes inaccurate due to a lack of medical knowledge and understanding.

What treatment was available for most medieval people?
There were 5 main ways in which you could get treatment:
- Rich people would consult a physician.
- There were hospitals, but people went to them for rest and prayer rather than medical intervention.
- Most people were cared for in the home by the women in their family.
- People could visit barber-surgeons to have simple surgical procedures.
- Apothecaries provided medicinal treatments using plants and herbs.

Why did women give medieval treatment in the home?
It cost money to see a physician and most people could not afford it.

How did medieval women give treatment at home?
Women used treatments that they learned from other women in their household. They would mix remedies using herbs from their gardens and do their best to make their patients comfortable. Women also acted as midwives at births.

What was the religious approach to treatment in medieval times?
As people believed that God created illnesses as a punishment for sinning, then the treatment involved a religious act such as fasting, paying for a special mass, prayer, or pilgrimage.

What was the supernatural approach to treatment in medieval times?
Using charms or chanting spells was believed to scare off illness and heal people. Astrology was also used, as physicians referred to star charts to determine when certain treatments could be carried out.

What was the humoural approach to treatment in medieval times?
Bloodletting, purging and the Theory of Opposites were used to help balance the humours.

What was the remedial approach to treatment in medieval times?
Herbal remedies were inhaled or drunk to treat illnesses. Sometimes bathing in water with flowers and herbs was encouraged as it was believed it could help balance the humours by removing blockages.

Where could the poor go for treatment in medieval England?

The poor could be treated by women in their home. They could also seek rest in a medieval hospital (p.24); but, although they would be made comfortable there, they would not receive medical treatment.

> **DID YOU KNOW?**
>
> **One reason why medieval hospitals were effective was because the Church had more access to clean water.**
>
> It could afford to pipe it down from fresh sources on high ground to wash its holy items, and to use in its ceremonies. It was probably also beneficial for the sick people who were cared for by the Church.

PREVENTION
Clean living, the medieval way

 How did people try to prevent illness in medieval times?

There were four main methods of prevention used in medieval times: religion, purifying the air, diet, and the regimen sanitatis.

 How did the medieval Church try to prevent illness?

The most important ways were trying to not commit any sins, praying regularly and paying tithes to the Church.

 How did people try to prevent miasma in medieval times?

People tried to purify the air to protect themselves from miasma. Local councils put measures in place to make sure the streets were cleaned.

 How did people use diet to prevent illness in medieval times?

People believed if you ate too much it could cause an imbalance of humours, so people often used to purge themselves as a way to treat this.

 How did physicians try to prevent illness in medieval times?

Physicians would write instructions, called the regimen sanitatis, for healthy living. It was only used by the rich as it was very expensive: it would instruct them to take baths and make sure their houses were clean.

> **DID YOU KNOW?**
>
> **Regimen Sanitatis often advised people to avoid stress.**
>
> Some of the advice given was to avoid barking dogs, drunk people, and arguments with neighbours.

HOSPITALS
Providing health care, shelter and hospitality

What were medieval hospitals like?
In medieval times, hospitals were mostly run by the Church, with monks and nuns to care for patients.

How were people cared for in medieval hospitals?
Hospitals were focused on caring for patients, not curing them. Monks and nuns kept patients comfortable, and made sure their beds faced the hospital's altar.

Who did medieval hospitals look after?
Hospitals cared for different types of people in medieval times.
- Hospitals for lepers were set up. These hospitals were not inside towns, but were on the outskirts, as lepers were considered outcasts.
- Medieval hospitals were also used to house the poor and elderly.
- Hospitals that did care for the infirm only provided basic nursing.

DID YOU KNOW?
47% of medieval hospitals were almshouses, which cared for the poor and the destitute.

PHYSICIANS
Physicians were the doctors of the medieval period

What were medieval doctors prohibited from doing?
Physicians who were monks were not permitted to dissect dead bodies or carry out treatment that would involve cutting a patient. This led to bloodletting and other surgeries being carried out by barber surgeons.

What training did medieval doctors have?
Medical training was arduous, with a medical degree taking seven to ten years to complete. Potential doctors studied the works of Hippocrates *(p.20)* and Galen *(p.21)*. Very few had the chance to dissect a body. As there weren't many physicians, seeing one cost a lot of money.

What was the role of the medieval Church in training doctors?
Many universities were funded by the Catholic Church, which meant their teaching was influenced by the Church's beliefs.

What methods did medieval doctors use?
Medieval physicians used 4 main treatment methods:
- Diagnosis. Medieval physicians rarely treated patients themselves. Instead they would carry out a diagnosis and recommend a course of treatment to be carried out by a barber surgeon *(p.26)* or an apothecary. *(p.25)*
- Sample study. Physicians would study their patients' blood, urine and faeces to reach a diagnosis.

- Astrology. Physicians would look at astrological charts to see how the stars were aligned when their patient was born and when they fell ill.
- Study of 'humoural *(p. 19)* tendencies'. These were personality traits believed to be linked to your humours. For example, a quick-tempered person was believed to have too much yellow bile.

Why did not many people visit a medieval physician?

Most doctors were based in large towns, and even so there weren't many of them. Consulting them was expensive, so most people could not afford to see them.

> **DID YOU KNOW?**
>
> **Urology was the study of urine to make a diagnosis.**
> Medieval physicians would diagnose a patient by examining their urine to identify the humoural imbalance. This involved testing the appearance, colour, smell and taste of the urine.

APOTHECARIES
The person who mixed herbal remedies

What were apothecaries?

Apothecaries were people who sold herbal remedies. They had good knowledge of the healing powers of plants and herbs.

How did apothecaries train?

Apothecaries were not trained at university, instead they gained most of their knowledge from family members and through experience. Many also used a book called 'Materia Medica' to study herbal remedies.

Who visited apothecaries?

As many people were too poor to see a physician, they would visit an apothecary instead as their services were much cheaper. As a result, apothecaries were viewed as rivals to their businesses by physicians.

> **DID YOU KNOW?**
>
> **Unlike physicians, apothecaries did not take the Hippocratic Oath.**
> This meant that they were not bound by the instruction to do no harm, and might mix poisons if they were asked to do so.

MEDIEVAL SURGERY
Surgery was extremely dangerous in the medieval period

What was surgery like during medieval times?
Surgery in medieval times was backwards, dangerous and very few patients survived.

What were the problems with surgery in medieval times?
There were 3 main problems with surgery in medieval times:

- Pain: the pain was excruciating and there were no real anaesthetics. Natural anaesthetics like hemlock or opium were used to numb pain, but they were dangerous as a high doses could kill the patient. The pain could be so bad that some patients died of shock.
- Infection: because there was no understanding of what caused them, many patients died from post-surgery infections. Many doctors believed that the presence of pus in wounds helped patients recover. Dirty surgical instruments were seen as a sign of a surgeon's experience.
- Blood loss: blood transfusions did not exist and patients often lost a lot of blood during surgery, which could be fatal.

> **DID YOU KNOW?**
>
> **Henry V had a successful operation for an arrow-wound to the face, while he was the teenaged 'Prince Hal'.**
>
> The surgeon, John Bradmore, removed the arrow with special forceps and dressed the wound with barley and honey.

BARBER SURGEONS
Cutting off hair, and perhaps arms and legs

What were barber surgeons?
Barber surgeons were barbers who had no formal university training. They had access to sharp blades so performed some medical procedures, such as pulling teeth, and bleeding patients to treat some illnesses.

What medical procedures did barber surgeons perform?
Barber surgeons would usually carry out the following surgeries:

- They would pull teeth.
- They also performed minor surgeries and, in some cases, even amputations.
- Bloodletting.

What were the risks in using a barber-surgeon?
A lot of people died because their wounds became infected. Barber surgeons also often over-bled their patients which resulted in death.

> **DID YOU KNOW?**
>
> **Barber surgeons often kept a bowl of blood in their window to let people know what their business was.**
>
> Later, this was replaced by a red and white striped pole, representing a bloody and bandaged arm.

LEPROSY
Infectious and isolating

What was leprosy?
Leprosy was a painful skin disease which resulted in internal and external ulcers and the loss of hair, fingers and toes. Patients would suffer from paralysis and eventually die.

What did people believe about the causes of leprosy?
Many people believed that diseases were sent as a punishment by God. Leprosy was mentioned in the Bible and this made the belief more popular.

What was the cure for leprosy?
There was no cure for leprosy, so people were often cast out from communities. However, a few lazar houses were set up to help care for those with the illness.

How did people believe leprosy was spread?
People wrongly believed that the breath of a leper was contagious.

How did medieval people try to stop the spread of leprosy?
There were 3 main ways to prevent the spread of leprosy:
- Isolate lepers from the community by casting them out.
- They had to wear a cloak and frequently ring a bell if they were in towns. This was so that other people were warned of their presence.
- To ensure they remained at a distance from others, they were not allowed to enter narrow alleyways.

> **DID YOU KNOW?**
>
> **'Lazar houses' accounted for 31% of medieval hospitals.**
>
> Many people donated money to lazar houses as Catholics believed it could get a person through Purgatory and into Heaven more quickly. This was because lepers were believed to be living through Purgatory on earth.

BLACK DEATH
Catastrophe strikes in 1348

What was the Black Death?
The Black Death was an epidemic that hit England. It was the bubonic plague, a serious infection of the lymphatic system which caused buboes (pus-filled swellings) in the groin and armpits. People died within five days of becoming ill.

When did the Black Death arrive in England?
The Black Death arrived in England in 1348.

What did people think caused the Black Death?
People during the medieval period, people believed in 3 main causes of the Black Death:
- People thought it was caused by God, punishing people on earth for their sins.
- Some believed it was due to miasma (bad air).
- Astrologists blamed an unusual alignment of the planets in 1345, three years earlier.

How did the Black Death spread?
Bubonic plague was caused by bacteria in fleas' stomachs. Infected fleas were carried on the backs of rats to new places and then passed it to humans. The disease spread quickly because people lived close to each other at that time.

What did people do to stop themselves catching the Black Death?
People used 4 key methods to treat the Black Death.
- They prayed for God's forgiveness. Many carried out flagellation (whipping) to show they were sorry. Many believed the Black Death was God's will, so there was no way to cure it.
- Carrying strong-smelling herbs to ward off miasma was recommended by physicians. It was also believed that lighting fires and boiling vinegar would also have the same effect.
- Apothecaries created herbal remedies to try and treat the disease. Many were mixtures that had to be applied directly to the buboes.
- Some recommended lancing the buboes to release the pus.

What measures were taken to stop the spread of the Black Death?
People tried to prevent the spread of the Black Death and stop themselves catching it in 4 main ways.
- Some towns built cemeteries away from people's homes, because they believed the dead bodies caused miasma that was infecting people.
- Towns tried to ban travellers from entering. Local governments introduced quarantine laws stating newcomers must spend 40 days apart from any other people. They also considered banning large gatherings such as church services.
- Street cleaning was stopped by some local governments because they believed the smell from rubbish and waste would drive away the miasma.
- People went on pilgrimages, prayed, fasted, and whipped themselves to show God they were sorry for their sins. They hoped God would forgive them and not strike them down with the Black Death.

What was the impact of the Black Death?
The Black Death had a lasting impact on England for the following 5 main reasons:
- It is estimated the Black Death killed around a third of the population of England.
- The shortage of labourers meant that peasants could travel to where conditions and pay were better.
- The balance of power shifted towards the poorest in society, as feudalism came to an end.

- People began to challenge the social hierarchy. As the rich and wealthy were not immune from the disease, they were therefore not seen as better than others.
- The Church was also not immune from the disease, as many clergymen died.

When did the Black Death end?
The worst of the Black Death was over by 1350. It returned many times over the following decades, but infected fewer people each time.

> **DID YOU KNOW?**
> The bacteria responsible for the plague is called Yersinia pestis.

MEDICINE - CHANGE & CONTINUITY
Very, very slow progress

How did medieval medicine change over time?
Medieval medicine changed little due to religious and superstitious beliefs. Overall, the medieval period hindered medical progress.

What were the main changes to medicine in the medieval period?
There were 2 main aspects of change for medicine during the medieval period.
- By the end of the period, there were some hospitals and a few doctors who would treat poor people.
- Although they did not do it regularly, governments started playing a role in public health, through ordering places to be cleaned.

What stayed the same for medicine during the medieval period?
There were 5 main aspects of continuity for medicine during the medieval period.
- In order to treat everyday illnesses most people still depended on the work of local healers and women in the home.
- Most people still used herbal remedies to cure diseases.
- People still believed in the Theory of the Four Humours, as the Church's influence was so strong nobody challenged ideas it supported or accepted.
- Surgery was limited as there were no effective anaesthetics. The most frequent surgeries performed were tooth extractions, bloodletting and amputations.
- Religion still played an important role in explaining why people got sick.

> **DID YOU KNOW?**
>
> **Physicians began to be commonly known as 'doctors' in the sixteenth century.**
>
> The word doctor was initially used in the 13th century by the universities of Bologna and Paris to describe people with medical training who were qualified to teach others.

RENAISSANCE
A period where many old ideas were disproved, but new ones were still being formed

What was the Renaissance?
Meaning 'rebirth', it was time of great artistic and scientific progress. It was a period of transition from the ancient to the modern world.

When was Renaissance?
The Renaissance has no set dates but but it is generally considered to be around 1400 - 1600 in northern Europe.

What were some of the main developments during the Renaissance?
There are 3 key consequences of the Renaissance:
- Gunpowder was discovered which made wars and battles more bloody and led to new types of wounds.
- The idea of humanism was developed. This is the belief that high levels of human potential could be achieved through education.
- Global exploration led to the discovery of new lands and cultures, and therefore new medicines.

What changed in medicine during the Renaissance?
Changes to people's attitudes and ways of thinking during the Renaissance also led to 5 main changes in medicine.
- The Theory of the Four Humours fell out of favour with physicians as they began to understand that disease was something separate from the body, not caused by a person's humours being out of balance.
- A much greater understanding of anatomy developed. Doctors were able to carry out more human dissections as the power of the Church declined, which meant they could correct assumptions and mistakes made by Galen *(p.21)* and others.
- Physicians no longer diagnosed patients from urine samples, and astrology also became less popular among medical professionals.
- Physicians came to rely more on their own observations, studies, and procedures such as dissections. They no longer relied on obtaining knowledge from books written by Galen *(p.21)* and other doctors, although these were still used to research symptoms.
- Most of the medical advances were in the field of anatomical study, not treatment or prevention.

In what ways did medicine not develop during the Renaissance?
Although the Renaissance was a time of great change there were 3 main aspects of medicine which stayed the same:
- Ordinary people still held the same beliefs as their medieval ancestors about what caused illness. The Church remained a powerful force among the poor, so many still believed sickness was a punishment from God.
- Ordinary people continued to rely on the same treatments for disease as their medieval ancestors, including the need to balance the four humours, and the part played by religion.
- Miasma theory remained. Both physicians and ordinary people continued to believe disease could be caused by bad air. This was because there was no alternative explanation at the time.

How did medical training improve during the Renaissance?
During the Renaissance, there were 3 key improvements in medical training.
- Although physicians continued to learn from books, they were taught some new ideas about anatomy and chemistry.
- Surgeons had to obtain a licence and were now allowed to perform dissections.
- Apothecaries were also now licensed to trade, and had more ingredients and recipes from around the world.

> **DID YOU KNOW?**
>
> **Soap wasn't readily available in the Renaissance.**
> Only really rich people could afford expensive olive oil soap. Most soap was made of animal fat and, although it was good for laundry, it was too harsh for the skin.

PRINTING PRESS
A technological change that had an impact on the spread of medical ideas

What was the printing press?
The printing press is a machine used to reproduce writing and images. It uses ink on paper to make many identical copies.

When was the printing press invented?
The first printing press was created around 1440, through early experiments in printing. A commercial machine was available by 1450.

Who invented the printing press?
Johannes *(p.32)* Gutenberg, a German goldsmith, is usually credited as the inventor of the printing press.

What was the significance of the printing press?
New ideas and medical knowledge could be spread more quickly due to the invention of the printing press.

Why was the printing press important for medicine?
There were 4 main reasons why the printing press was important in medicine.
- ☑ Publishing lots of copies of a theory meant many people had the chance to understand a theory in detail, and either object to or agree with it.
- ☑ Medical students were able to use books and manuals to help them learn.
- ☑ Books no longer had to be copied out by hand in monasteries, or only produced in Latin. It meant scientists could share information easily with each other.
- ☑ Control over what was published, and therefore which ideas influenced society, was no longer in the hands of the Church. This meant that the influence of Galen's *(p.21)* ideas was reduced.

> **DID YOU KNOW?**
>
> The first printing press was made from a wine press (used to press grapes for making wine).

Get our free app at GCSEHistory.com

JOHANNES GUTENBERG
German inventor of the printing-press

Who was Johannes Gutenberg?

Johannes Gutenberg invented the printing press *(p.31)* in the 1440s.

TREATMENTS
New ideas slowly make an impact

Did treatments in the Renaissance improve?

Diagnosis and treatment had not advanced much since the Middle Ages. Just as before, physicians did not know or understand what caused diseases or how to cure them.

In what ways were Renaissance treatments similar to previous periods?

Despite some advances, there will still 4 main aspects of continuity witnessed in Renaissance *(p.30)* medicine.
- People were still superstitious. It was believed that the touch of a king could cure people of diseases like scrofula.
- Doctors still hadn't understood the link between dirt and disease.
- There was continuity in ideas about what caused disease: for example, miasma.
- Herbal remedies remained popular.
- Bloodletting was still used as a treatment.

How did treatment change during the Renaissance?

There were 4 key changes that happened to medicine during the Renaissance *(p.30)* period.
- Galen *(p.21)* no longer dominated scientific thought, as doctors began to challenge his ideas.
- Technology was gradually advancing so that new inventions, like the microscope, helped make more discoveries.
- Alchemy became popular, as people began to look at using chemicals for cures, rather than balancing the humours.
- The Theory of Transference became popular. This suggested that a disease could be transferred through contact with a plant or animal. People might rub a vegetable on their ailments, in the hope that the vegetable would catch it and take it away.

DID YOU KNOW?

During the Renaissance, damp skin was believed to be more vulnerable to miasma.

As a result, people avoided getting sweaty, or using too much water to wash. They might instead 'dry wash' themselves with a piece of linen.

PREVENTION
The same ideas, but more government intervention

What were the methods of preventing disease during the Renaissance?
There were 6 main methods of prevention in the Renaissance period. These were religion, purifying the air, fasting, remedies from apothecaries, some government public health actions, and equipment for doctors (such as outfits to help combat the Plague).

How did people believe religion prevented illness during the Renaissance?
People were advised to pray to God and repent their sins.

How did people prevent miasma during the Renaissance?
People were advised to purify the air by carrying a pomander. This was a ball of sweet smelling herbs.

How was diet used to prevent illness during the Renaissance?
Fasting was advised, as well as garlic-heavy diets.

What did apothecaries do to prevent illness during the Renaissance?
Apothecaries provided herbal remedies such as chewing dry tobacco to ward off the miasma.

How did the government try to prevent illness during the Renaissance?
The government played a much bigger role in public health, through quarantine laws and street cleaning.

How did plague doctors try to prevent illness during the Renaissance?
Plague doctors wore special beak-shaped masks, and coated their coats in wax so that blood and pus did not stick to it.

> **DID YOU KNOW?**
>
> **Henry VIII closed down public baths - called 'stewes' - during his reign.**
>
> They were believed to cause the spread of syphilis or 'the Great Pox'. As syphilis is an STD, and stewes were often used as brothels, there may have been some truth in this.

ROYAL SOCIETY
A hub of medical ideas and new thinking

What is the Royal Society?
The Royal Society was an English institution the purpose of which was to promote and support scientific research. Its members were a group of influential scientists, and it was created with the approval of King Charles II.

When was the Royal Society created?

The Royal Society was created in November 1660, and still exists today.

What was the purpose of the Royal Society?

The purpose of the Royal Society was to promote scientific understanding by sharing knowledge.

How did the Royal Society spread its ideas?

The Royal Society published a journal called 'Philosophical Transactions'. It contained experiments and research from scientists. The work was written in English rather than Latin, so that more people could understand it. The journal is still in publication today.

What was the motto of the Royal Society?

The motto of the Royal Society was 'Nullius in verba', which means 'Take nobody's word for it'.

Was the Royal Society credible?

People took notice of the Royal Society because King Charles II gave it a Royal Charter in 1662. Having the king's support gave it credibility.

DID YOU KNOW?

Robert Hooke, who invented the microscope, was the original Curator of Experiments for the Royal Society.

ANDREAS VESALIUS

The father of modern anatomy

Who was Vesalius?

Andreas Vesalius was a Belgian physician. He trained at the universities of Louvain, Paris and Padua.

How did Vesalius make new discoveries?

Vesalius made many discoveries through dissection and by recording his discoveries in anatomical drawings. He stole bodies from cemeteries and gallows to dissect them, as well as dissecting the corpses of criminals.

What did Vesalius discover?

He identified approximately 300 mistakes in Galen's *(p.21)* work, including that:
- ✔ The human jawbone is formed from a single part, not two.
- ✔ Women do not have one more pair of ribs than men do.
- ✔ The human breast bone does not have 7 parts; it has 3 parts.

Why was Vesalius controversial?

Vesalius used dissections to show how Galen's *(p.21)* understanding of the human body was incorrect. This subsequently lost Vesalius his job at the university.

What was Vesalius's famous book?
Vesalius is most famous because of his book 'On the Fabric of the Human Body' which was published in 1543. The drawings of human anatomy in the book were exceptionally detailed.

Why was Vesalius significant?
Vesalius was very important for Renaissance *(p.30)* medicine for 4 main reasons.
- His work encouraged other doctors to question the old medical books and to learn through first-hand experience by performing dissections.
- His studies of the circulatory system were an important contribution to the understanding that the heart acts as a pump.
- The illustrations in 'On the Fabric of the Human Body' were copied and inserted into other books.
- Others were able to develop his work into the human anatomy further, because he provided the detailed ground work.

How was Vesalius's work brought to England?
Vesalius's work was transformed into a new book by Thomas Geminus called the 'Compendiosa'. All of his illustrations were copied and paired with surgical knowledge. This book became popular in England and was used by barber-surgeons.

DID YOU KNOW?

In the original Latin, Vesalius's book was called 'De Humani Corporis Fabrica Libri Septem'.

WILLIAM HARVEY
Identifying the circulation of the blood

Who was William Harvey?
William Harvey was an English doctor who studied medicine at university in Cambridge and Padua. He specialised in physiology, and was physician to both James I and Charles I in England.

How did Harvey challenge the work of Galen?
He challenged Galen's *(p.21)* understanding that blood was made in the liver and that it was used as fuel. Harvey believed blood circulated around the body. This marked the beginning of the end of Galen's superiority.

How did Harvey explain blood circulation?
Harvey demonstrated how the heart was a pump for moving blood around the body. He used valves from a dissected heart to demonstrate that blood could only flow in one direction.

What were the limitations of Harvey's understanding of blood circulation?
Harvey's understanding of blood circulation was limited in 2 main ways.
- He did not understand why blood needed to circulate around the body.
- He did not know why blood in the arteries was different from blood in the veins.

Why did Harvey face resistance from other doctors?

Harvey made a major discovery, but the medical community was resistant to change for 3 key reasons.

- Blood transfusions to combat blood loss were now attempted, as Harvey's work demonstrated that this was essential. These attempts failed because there was a lack of understanding of blood groups. Therefore, his work was seen as not having much practical application.
- After so many years of Church dominance, during which Galen's *(p.21)* theories ruled medical understanding, people were reluctant to accept alternative information.
- As Harvey did not know why blood needed to circulate, or why the blood in arteries and veins was different, some other doctors rejected his ideas.

What was the significance of Harvey's work?

His theory of circulation was the first step towards blood transfusions becoming possible, and therefore saving lives. He was also one of the first to question Galen *(p.21)*. However, his impact at the time was small.

Which factors contributed to Harvey's discovery?

There were 4 main factors that helped Harvey's discovery.

- As an individual, Harvey was skilled, and was employed by Charles I. This gave him credibility and popularity.
- Institutions such as the Church were declining in popularity and influence, which meant that more people were challenging Galen's *(p.21)* work.
- Harvey was inspired by new technology, such as the mechanical water pump.
- Attitudes in society were changing. People were seeking scientific explanations during the Renaissance *(p.30)*. This influenced medicine in terms of people's understanding of the body, and the diagnosis and treatment of illness.

How did people react to Harvey's discovery?

People reacted to Harvey's discovery in 4 main ways.

- Some criticised Harvey and said that he was mad to suggest that blood circulated in the body.
- His ideas went against Galen *(p.21)*, and some doctors refused to support him as a result.
- French anatomist Jean Riolan called Harvey a 'circulator', which meant that he was a 'quack'.
- Although some opposed him, his theory was accepted by many during his life.

DID YOU KNOW?

Harvey struggled to find acceptance for his theories.
They caused a loss of reputation and his business dropped as a result. He himself later called them his 'crackpot ideas'.

THOMAS SYDENHAM
Identifying disease as a group of symptoms, rather than an imbalance in the individual

Who was Thomas Sydenham?

Thomas Sydenham was an English physician who advanced the use scientific processes in medicine.

What was Thomas Sydenham also known as?
Sydenham was known as 'the English Hippocrates *(p.20)*'.

What was Thomas Sydenham's main idea?
Sydenham would not rely on medical books alone. He believed in observing the patients and recording their symptoms. This process allowed him to see patterns between illnesses and treatments.

What was the main contribution of Thomas Sydenham?
Sydenham classified diseases into different types, based on which symptoms each patient exhibited. He was able to show, for example, that measles and scarlet fever were different types of disease.

What was the name of Thomas Sydenham's book?
In 1676, Sydenham published 'Medical Observations'. It explained how illnesses and diseases had external causes, and were not the result of something internal such as unbalanced humours.

What was the significance of Thomas Sydenham?
Sydenham was important because he paved the way for future doctors to take a more scientific approach to medicine.

DID YOU KNOW?

Sydenham has been called 'the English Hippocrates'.
This was because he emphasised careful observations of the patient and detailed record-keeping.

HOSPITALS - CHANGE & CONTINUITY
Closed down by the English Reformation

What were hospitals like in the Renaissance?
Some hospitals during the Renaissance *(p.30)* were still controlled by the Church, but fewer than before. They were very different from the hospitals that existed previously.

How did hospitals change during the Renaissance?
During the Renaissance *(p.30)*, hospitals changed in 6 key ways.
- Hospitals were no longer just places where pilgrims, travellers and the elderly could rest and pray. Patients were given treatment, and records were kept to show how many people recovered.
- Physicians started to visit patients in the hospitals, where they carried out observations and recommended treatments.
- Hospitals began to have their own apothecaries and pharmacies to make medicines.
- Hospitals began to provide good food for patients to eat. Although it was no longer believed that diet affected the four humours, it was accepted that it was important to recover and maintain good health.
- People began to visit hospitals when they sustained injuries in order to have them treated.
- As King Henry VIII closed down monasteries during the Reformation, many hospitals also closed as they were run by the Church. It took some time for numbers to increase again, and many hospitals were subsequently run by charities.

PEST HOUSES
Special hospitals for infectious diseases

What were pest houses?
Pest houses were set up for people suffering from extremely infectious diseases, like the plague.

GREAT PLAGUE
A major epidemic in London

What was the Great Plague?
The Great Plague was the last major epidemic of bubonic plague in England.

When was the Great Plague?
The Great Plague lasted from 1665 to 1666.

How many people died during the Great Plague?
The Great Plague killed 100,000 people, almost a quarter of London's population.

What did people believe were the causes of the Great Plague?
Due to a lack of medical understanding at the time, there were 3 main theories about the causes of the Great Plague.
- People believed that God had sent the disease as punishment.
- People believed that miasmas or bad smells caused the disease.
- Many believed that an unusual alignment of planets caused the disease.

What were the remedies used against the Great Plague?
Measures and cures for the plague were often unusual and extreme and included 5 main measures.
- Physicians tried to balance their patients' humours, for example by bloodletting.
- Fires were lit in the streets to purify the air.
- Infected houses were quarantined. A red cross, and the words 'God have mercy upon us', were painted on the door.
- Public prayer and confession.
- Transference was also carried out: for example, by attaching a live chicken to the buboes.

How were quack doctors involved in the plague?
Quack doctors were people who had no medical training, but who charged people for treatment as if they were a physician or apothecary. *(p.25)*

What were the quack cures during the Great Plague?
Due to a lack of medical understanding, there were a number of quack cures for the Great Plague. Quack doctors sold different pills or herbal remedies that supposedly cured people, or protected them from the disease.

How did the government intervene to try to stop the spread the Great Plague?

The government enforced 5 key measures to try and prevent the disease spreading.

- They banned public meetings, fairs, and large funerals.
- Streets and alleyways were regularly cleaned.
- Dogs and cats were killed, because people believed they were spreading the disease.
- Plague victims had to be quarantined for 40 days.
- Carts travelled through the city to collect dead bodies.

 What event is believed to have helped end the great plague?

Some people believe the Great Fire of London killed much of the plague bacteria, by killing the rats who carried the fleas which transmitted the disease.

 What new methods had been made since the Black Death to limit the spread of the Great Plague?

There were 5 important improvements made since the Black Death *(p.28)*, that helped fight the Great Plague.

- People began to recognise the connection between dirt and disease.
- Trade was stopped, and mass gatherings were banned.
- The England-Scotland border was closed, helping to limit the spread of the disease.
- Quarantine was more effective, as people stayed in their houses to stop the disease spreading.
- Dead bodies were collected, and buried in 'plague' pits' that were six feet deep.

> **DID YOU KNOW?**
>
> **During the Great Plague, Charles II and his advisors escaped London to the countryside.**
>
> For the eight months that they were there, while 100,000 Londoners died, they had three meetings about the plague. Two were about how they could keep the king safe.

GREAT PLAGUE & BLACK DEATH COMPARED
How much had changed in three hundred years?

 Were there similarities and differences between the Black Death and the Great Plague?

Despite being separated by over 300 years, there were many similarities between the Black Death *(p.28)* of 1348 and the Great Plague *(p.38)* in 1665. This was because there had been very few medical developments that helped to explain the connection between germs and disease.

 What were the similarities between the Black Death and the Great Plague?

There were 3 main similarities between the Black Death *(p.28)* and the Great Plague *(p.38)*.

- Many still believed that God sent the disease as a punishment, or that it was caused by miasma.
- Many people moved to the countryside to avoid the larger, cramped cities.
- There was no cure for the disease, as doctors didn't understand the connection between germs and diseases.

What were the differences between the Black Death and the Great Plague?
There were also 4 main differences between the Black Death (p.28) and the Great Plague (p.38).

- Methods of preventing the spread of the plague in 1665 were more carefully planned, and the Mayor of London did more to help.
- During the Great Plague (p.38), residents were ordered to sweep the streets in front of their houses, making the environment cleaner.
- When a person died, plague-searchers were sent to examine bodies and determine whether they had died from the plague. Their diagnosis was later confirmed by surgeons.
- In 1665, doctors and scientists had better understanding of the connection between dirt and disease, although they couldn't explain it.

> **DID YOU KNOW?**
>
> **Historians don't always agree about the type of plague that caused the Black Death.**
>
> The descriptions of symptoms fit bubonic plague. However, the epidemic became worse in winter and archaeological evidence suggests that there were fewer rats than expected. These details don't fit if the disease was spread by fleas.

LAISSEZ-FAIRE
Let it be ...

What was laissez-faire?
Laissez-faire, a French term that translates as 'let it be', was the idea that the government should take a hands-off approach to public health.

BELIEF IN CAUSES OF DISEASE - CHANGE & CONTINUITY
New ideas gather pace

What was the understanding of disease in the 19th century?
In the mid-nineteenth century, understanding of disease was based on miasma and spontaneous generation.

What did people believe about miasma and disease in the 19th century?
People still believed that disease was carried through bad air.

What was the understanding of spontaneous generation in the 19th century?
Spontaneous generation was a theory that rotting material - such as food and excrement - created microorganisms, which caused miasma and disease.

Why did the understanding of disease not progress in the 19th century?

There were 2 main factors affecting medical progress and understanding in the mid-nineteenth century.
- Hospitals relied on charity for funding. There was generally little money available for research.
- Doctors wanted to continue to work as they always had, and were reluctant to try new methods for treating patients.

What were the main changes that led to understanding disease in the nineteenth century?

There were 5 main changes that allowed for medical progress in the 19th century.
- The development of microscopes allowed Louis Pasteur *(p.43)* to develop and publish his germ theory *(p.43)* in 1861.
- Supernatural *(p.18)* and religious ideas about disease were dying out.
- More hospitals were built, and the work of Florence Nightingale *(p.46)* meant they were a lot cleaner.
- The development of anaesthetics and antiseptics led to improvements in surgery.
- The government began to take more action and implemented measures to improve public health.

> **DID YOU KNOW?**
>
> **There were 'cholera riots' during the first cholera outbreak in 1831.**
>
> People were angry at having their movement limited, and being unable to visit their loved ones in cholera hospitals.

INOCULATION

Smallpox inoculation was introduced to Britain by Lady Mary Montagu in 1723.

What was inoculation?

One method of prevention was inoculation. This involved putting pus from an infected person's scab into a cut on a healthy person's body. This allowed the body to develop natural resistance to the infection, protecting it in future: it would become 'inoculated'.

What were the problems with inoculation?

Although inoculation did sometimes protect people from smallpox, there were 3 main problems with its use.
- It was dangerous. Although inoculated patients usually only got a mild dose of smallpox, there was no guarantee of this. Sometimes they developed a severe case that could kill them.
- Patients were contagious after being inoculated, and might infect other people. They were supposed to spend some time in quarantine afterwards.
- It was offered by high-status doctors, who might charge as much as £20 for an inoculation (the equivalent of about £1,500 in today's money). This meant that it just wasn't available to ordinary people.

> **DID YOU KNOW?**
>
> **Smallpox inoculation was introduced to Britain by Lady Mary Montagu in 1723.**
>
> She learnt the procedure in Istanbul, where she was inoculated against a smallpox epidemic that killed her brother.

EDWARD JENNER AND VACCINATION
The 'Father of Immunology'

Who was Edward Jenner?
Edward Jenner was a country doctor who discovered vaccines.

What was Jenner known as?
Jenner was also known as 'the Father of Immunology'.

What was used before Jenner created vaccinations?
Inoculation *(p.41)* involved spreading the pus from an infected wound into a cut on the skin of a healthy person. They would then catch a mild case of the disease and build up immunity.

What disease did Jenner help cure?
In the 18th century, smallpox was a big killer. It was highly infectious and spread from one person to another through coughing, sneezing or touching. It killed about 30% of the people who caught it.

What did Jenner observe?
In the 1790s, Jenner realised that milkmaids did not catch smallpox if they had already had cowpox.

What was Jenner's experiment?
Jenner's experiment involved deliberately infecting a boy with cowpox, then later infecting him with smallpox. The boy didn't catch smallpox as he had built up resistance to it.

Why was vaccination safer than inoculation according to Jenner?
Vaccination against smallpox proved that you didn't need to catch a disease directly in order to build up immunity to it. Jenner simply used a similar and milder disease, cowpox, to help protect against smallpox.

When did Jenner publish his theory on vaccination?
Jenner published his theory in 1798.

Why did Jenner call his discovery vaccination?
The name vaccine comes from the Latin word vacca, which means cow.

Why did Jenner face opposition to his discovery?
There were 6 main reasons Jenner faced opposition.

- ☑ The Church did not believe cows should play a part in healing humans, seeing it as unnatural.
- ☑ Inoculation *(p.41)* doctors were angry, because inoculation was an expensive treatment that made them a lot of money. Vaccination would take away this income.
- ☑ Jenner was not well known in London, as he was a country doctor. As a result, many were reluctant to believe his findings. The Royal Society *(p.33)* refused to publish them.
- ☑ Dr William Woodville was in dispute with Jenner after some of his patients died from smallpox while using Jenner's techniques. However, Woodville's equipment was later shown to be contaminated.
- ☑ Jenner published his findings, but could not explain how vaccination worked. This made it difficult for other doctors to accept his theory.

- ☑ This discovery was made before germ theory *(p.43)*, so Jenner couldn't explain the link between cowpox and smallpox or reproduce the link with any other diseases.

Why was Jenner significant?

Jenner was significant for 2 main reasons:
- ☑ His smallpox vaccine was the first successful vaccine to be developed and led to the science of immunology.
- ☑ In 1852, the vaccine was made compulsory and in 1980, the World Health Organisation declared that smallpox had been eradicated.

> **DID YOU KNOW?**
> Edward Jenner was a keen fossil-collector.

LOUIS PASTEUR'S GERM THEORY

'Chance only favours prepared minds'. Louis Pasteur

Who was Louis Pasteur?

Louis Pasteur was a French scientist who discovered germs and proved a direct connection between germs and disease.

When was Pasteur's germ theory published?

Louis Pasteur published his work on germ theory in 1861. In 1878, he published the next stage of his theory - that germs caused infection.

What was Pasteur's germ theory?

This was the theory that germs caused disease. It disproved previous beliefs about other causes, such as miasma.

What are the principles Pasteur's theory?

There were four basic principles of germ theory.
- ☑ The air contains living microorganisms.
- ☑ Microbes in the air cause decay.
- ☑ Microbes are not evenly distributed in the air.
- ☑ Microbes can be killed by heating them.

What led to Pasteur's germ theory?

In 1857, Pasteur was employed by a French brewery to work out why their beer kept going sour.

How did Pasteur make his discovery?

Using a microscope, he discovered microorganisms growing in the liquid. He realised that sterilising water, and keeping it in a sealed flask, prevented microorganisms from entering it. If the sterilised water was kept in an open flask, the microbes would breed again.

What was Pasteur's process of 'pasteurisation'?
Pasteur called the process of heating liquid to kill bacteria 'pasteurisation'.

How did Pasteur make the link between germs and disease?
In 1865, Pasteur was asked to investigate a problem in the silk industry. He discovered that silkworms were dying from microorganisms and subsequently made the link between germs and disease.

Why did doctors oppose Pasteur's theory?
Because microorganisms could be seen everywhere, for example in human blood, doctors could not understand why some caused disease and others did not.

What was the impact of Pasteur's germ theory?
There were 4 main results of germ theory.
- ☑ It demonstrated the belief that disease was created by spontaneous generation was wrong. However, spontaneous generation was still an influential idea that some doctors, such as Dr Henry Bastian, still supported.
- ☑ Between 1876 and 1883, Robert Koch *(p.45)* discovered that different bacteria cause different diseases.
- ☑ It led to an understanding of why infection occurred in surgery.
- ☑ It led to Lister's *(p.54)* use of carbolic acid *(p.53)* as an antiseptic *(p.53)* in surgery.

How did Pasteur discover a vaccine for chicken cholera?
The chicken cholera *(p.59)* vaccine was discovered by chance in 1879. A mistake by Pasteur's assistant led to the realisation that the germ was weakened when exposed to air. Injecting the weakened germ into chickens stopped them from catching the disease.

How did Pasteur help the development of vaccines?
Pasteur helped discover two other vaccines.
- ☑ In 1881, Pasteur's team produced a weakened strain of anthrax that would prevent the disease in sheep.
- ☑ In 1885, Pasteur successfully cured a boy from rabies by using a vaccine for the disease he had developed.

How did Pasteur's rivalry with Koch lead to scientific breakthroughs?
There are 5 main reasons why the rivalry between Pasteur and Koch *(p.45)* led to scientific breakthroughs.
- ☑ Both were researching during the Franco-Prussian War, and defeating diseases could have a big impact on the battlefield.
- ☑ The governments of France and Germany paid for the laboratories and teams of scientists, for Pasteur and Koch *(p.45)* respectively.
- ☑ The individual characters of both men played a role. Both were relentless in their attempts to make scientific advances. For Pasteur, this resulted in his scientific breakthrough about germ theory; and for Koch *(p.45)* it resulted in his discoveries about tuberculosis (TB) and cholera *(p.59)*.
- ☑ Communication increased the rivalry, as Koch *(p.45)* heard about Pasteur's discoveries quickly, helping him to make breakthroughs of his own.
- ☑ Teamwork and rivalry contributed to breakthroughs, as both sides quickly wanted to discover vaccinations for contagious diseases such as diphtheria. *(p.76)*

DID YOU KNOW?

Three of Louis Pasteur's five children died of typhoid.

ROBERT KOCH
Taking germ theory to the next level

Who was Robert Koch?
Robert Koch was a German doctor considered to be the founder of modern bacteriology.

What were Koch's achievements?
Koch's work was important for 3 main reasons.
- He developed a method for staining and photographing microorganisms using dye.
- He discovered the specific germs that caused a number of diseases: anthrax in 1876, tuberculosis in 1882, and cholera *(p.59)* in 1883.
- He developed the use of agar jelly for growing bacterial cultures on which he could experiment.
- He developed a steam steriliser which used heat to sterilise equipment and dressings.

How did Koch prove that cholera was spread through contaminated water?
In 1884, he found cholera *(p.59)* in drinking water in Calcutta, India, which proved it was spread in water supplies. This confirmed John Snow's *(p.60)* theory of why cholera had spread in London in 1854.

What was the significance of Koch's work?
Koch's work was a major breakthrough and he had 2 key impacts on medicine.
- Doctors began to study disease itself, rather than studying and treating symptoms.
- He made it easier for other scientists to identify and study bacteria, such as diphtheria *(p.76)* and pneumonia, because of his staining technique.

Why were Koch and Pasteur rivals?
Koch and Pasteur *(p.43)* were rivals for two key reasons:
- They fell out at an 1882 conference over a mistranslated term in Pasteur's *(p.43)* lecture. Two of Koch's students then wrote a long paper criticising Pasteur's findings on anthrax.
- Their countries were at war between 1870-71, and their respective governments gave them funding for research and equipment.

DID YOU KNOW?

Koch was a childhood prodigy
He taught himself to read newspapers when he was only 5, he loved to read the classics, and also became an expert in chess.

C18TH HOSPITALS - CHANGE & CONTINUITY
More endowments mean better health care

How many hospitals were there in the 18th century?
During the English Reformation many hospitals were closed. There were just five hospitals in England by 1700.

Who funded 18th century hospitals?
In the 1700s a number of new hospitals were built which were often funded by wealthy businessmen. Guy's Hospital in London was funded in 1724 by Thomas Guy, an investor in the South Sea Company. The hospital is still open today.

How were 18th century hospitals an improvement over previous centuries?
There were 4 main changes to hospitals during this period.
- ✅ The sick were properly cared for, unlike during medieval times, when hospitals were just a place for them to rest.
- ✅ Doctors received proper training, as medical schools were often attached to hospitals.
- ✅ Individual wards were developed to care for those with different types of diseases and illnesses.
- ✅ Hospitals now included an apothecary *(p.25)* and a surgeon.

What specialist hospitals were developed in the 18th century?
The 18th century saw not only the development of general hospitals for the sick, but also specialist hospitals.
- ✅ In 1746, London's Lock Hospital for venereal (sexually transmitted) diseases was opened.
- ✅ In 1747, wards in Middlesex Hospital were designated specifically for pregnant women.
- ✅ In 1751, St Luke's Hospital became the second largest public hospital for the mentally ill.

What impact did the changes to hospitals in the 18th century have?
These changes to hospitals had 3 main impacts.
- ✅ By 1800, over 20,000 patients per year were treated at hospitals in London.
- ✅ People's thinking about illness and poverty shifted, and caring for those who were sick became more of a priority.
- ✅ The thinking developed that an evidence-based, scientific approach could conquer illness.

DID YOU KNOW?

In 2020, Guy's Hospital employed 17,100 members of staff.

FLORENCE NIGHTINGALE
The Lady with the Lamp

Who was Florence Nightingale?
Born in 1820, Florence Nightingale became a nurse despite opposition from her family. She cared for patients during the Crimean War, and is often to referred to as the 'Lady with the Lamp'.

What was nursing and hospital care like before Florence Nightingale?
In the early 1800s, most people were cared for by family in their own homes. A doctor would visit the patient and prescribe them medicine. Nurses were untrained and did not keep records on patient care.

Why did Nightingale's family not want her to become a nurse?
Prior to Florence Nightingale's influence in the mid-nineteenth century, nursing had a bad reputation, and nurses required no skills or training.

What did Florence Nightingale do in the Crimean War?
In 1854, during the Crimean War, she went to the Scutari Hospital Barracks in Turkey with a team of 38 nurses, to care for wounded soldiers.

 ### What problems did Florence Nightingale face upon arrival in the Crimea?
Conditions were terrible for the 10,000 patients, and disease and infection were widespread. Medical supplies were limited, wards were filthy and infested with pests, and the food was poor.

 ### What were Florence Nightingale's contributions to medicine?
She implemented measures that significantly improved hygiene at Scutari. This included cleaning surfaces, washing bedding, and ensuring the kitchens were clean. The quality of the food given to patients was improved, and windows were opened to allow air to circulate.

 ### Why did Florence Nightingale make changes at Scutari?
Nightingale believed that miasmas were the cause of illness and that they would be prevented by keeping places clean.

 ### What impact did Florence Nightingale's actions have at Scutari?
It's believed her actions resulted in the death rate falling from 42% to just 2%. She also became very popular both in the hospital and back in Britain.

 ### What happened when Florence Nightingale returned from war?
Press coverage of her work in Scutari made Florence Nightingale famous. When she returned to Britain in 1856 she was considered an expert on nursing and hospitals.

 ### What were Florence Nightingale's achievements?
Florence Nightingale's achievements after she returned from Scutari included writing over 200 books and creating training schools for nurses.
- In 1859, she wrote the book 'Notes on Nursing', which became a bestseller.
- The Nightingale Fund was created, which raised over £44,000. She used the money to set up a training school at St Thomas's Hospital in 1860, and a training school for midwives at King's College Hospital in 1861.
- She played an important role in promoting the French pavilion-design of hospitals, with wider open spaces to prevent miasma, which made them cleaner and safer.

 ### What impact did Florence Nightingale have on hospitals?
In 'Notes from Nursing', Florence Nightingale set out her ideas about how hospitals were organised.
- She recommended building hospitals using a design developed in France. The design was based around the pavilion system, to ensure good ventilation through the wards which separated patients, in order to prevent the spread of contagious diseases.
- She suggested large windows to let in light and air.
- She also suggested surfaces should be easier to clean, such as tiled floors and painted walls.
- In 1868, St Thomas' Hospital (where the Nightingale School of Nurses was located) was rebuilt according to Nightingale's recommendations.

 ### What changes did Florence Nightingale bring to nursing?
There were 4 important changes that Florence Nightingale brought to nursing.
- In 1860, Florence Nightingale opened the Nightingale School For Nurses at St Thomas' Hospital.

- This introduced strict rules for nurses - they had to go to bed at a certain time, and write a report on their progress every week.
- It gave nurses a formal training.
- It raised the status of nursing to a popular profession. By 1900, there were 68,000 trained nurses in Britain.

Why is Nightingale significant?

Florence Nightingale is regarded the founder of modern nursing. She turned nursing into a respectable profession, and introduced patient care and cleanliness to hospitals.

> **DID YOU KNOW?**
>
> **Florence Nightingale did not support the idea of female doctors.**
> Writing about them in 1860, she said that they 'have only tried to be men and have only succeeded in becoming third-rate men'.

SURGERY IN THE C19TH
Speed is replaced by anaesthetics, antiseptics and aseptics

What was surgery like in the nineteenth century?
Surgery in the mid-19th century was basic, dangerous, and had a low survival rate.

Why did so many people die in surgery before the late nineteenth century?
Surgery in the mid-19th century had a high mortality rate for 3 main reasons.
- It was painful, which caused some patients to go into shock and die. It was also hard for them to keep still, and surgeons had to work very fast, which increased the likelihood of mistakes.
- The wounds created by surgery were likely to become infected.
- Many patients bled to death.

What pain relief was used for surgery at the beginning of the nineteenth century?
Surgeons used various methods to try and prevent pain in the mid-nineteenth century. These included knocking patients out, giving them alcohol to make them drunk, or giving them opium. None were effective.

What was surgery like in the early nineteenth century?
Patients would usually be held down, and the operation performed as quickly as possible to reduce the amount of pain experienced. Operations often took place in the patient's home.

Why did surgery improve in the late nineteenth century?
The 19th century experienced 4 key changes for surgery.
- In 1861, Louis Pasteur *(p.43)* discovered that diseases were caused by germs, paving the way for antiseptic *(p.53)*, and later aseptic, surgery *(p.55)*.
- Joseph Lister's *(p.54)* carbolic acid *(p.53)* spray in 1865 killed germs before and during surgery, reducing infection with antiseptic *(p.53)* surgery.

- James Blundell *(p.49)* carried out early blood transfusions, publishing his paper 'Experiments on the Transfusion of Blood by the Syringe' in 1818.
- In 1847, James Simpson's *(p.53)* discovery of chloroform *(p.51)* reduced pain in surgery, particularly for childbirth.

> **DID YOU KNOW?**
>
> In the 1812 Battle of Borodino, the French surgeon Dominique-Jean Larrey apparently amputated 200 limbs in 24 hours.

ROBERT LISTON
'The fastest knife in the West End'

Who was Robert Liston?

Robert Liston was a surgeon renowned for his speed and strength. He once amputated a leg in 28 seconds. Liston was the first to use ether *(p.51)* as an anaesthetic *(p.49)* during surgery.

JAMES BLUNDELL
The first doctor to patent blood transfusions

Who is James Blundell?

James Blundell carried out early blood transfusions, publishing his paper 'Experiments on the Transfusion of Blood by the Syringe' in 1818.

ANAESTHETICS
Finding a solution to the problem of pain in surgery

What were anaesthetics?

Anaesthetics were developed during the 1800s to make surgery less painful for the patient.

What types of anaesthetics were used in the nineteenth century?

The use of 3 significant anaesthetics were developed in the nineteenth century:

- Nitrous oxide *(p.50)*.
- Ether *(p.51)*.
- Chloroform *(p.51)*.

> **DID YOU KNOW?**
>
> **Humphry Davy discovered the properties of nitrous oxide as a teenaged chemist.**
>
> He went on to use it recreationally with friends, and it was thirty years before it was introduced in medicine.

NITROUS OXIDE
Laughing gas

What was nitrous oxide?

Nitrous oxide, also known as laughing gas *(p.93)*, is an anaesthetic *(p.49)*. It was considered too weak to be suitable for major surgical operations.

Who discovered nitrous oxide?

Humphry Davy *(p.50)* discovered the anaesthetic *(p.49)* properties of nitrous oxide, although it was American dentist Horace Wells who first used it as an anaesthetic to extract a tooth.

When was nitrous oxide first used as an anaesthetic?

Nitrous oxide was first used as an anaesthetic *(p.49)* in 1844.

> **DID YOU KNOW?**
>
> **Horace Wells, an American dentist, suffered a humiliating failure when he tried to demonstrate nitrous oxide as an anaesthetic.**
>
> ✓ The patient cried out during the public tooth extraction at Harvard, so onlookers believed that he had failed. Wells was humiliated, and became addicted to chloroform after self-experimenting.
>
> ✓ The effects of his addiction caused him to throw acid at two people, and he committed suicide while in prison.

HUMPHRY DAVY
Famous chemist

Who was Humphry Davy?

Humphry Davy was a chemist and inventor, who discovered the use of nitrous oxide *(p.50)* as an anaesthetic. *(p.49)*

> **DID YOU KNOW?**
>
> **As a chemist, Davy invented a new type of science called electrochemistry**
>
> He used it to isolate new elements, such as potassium and sodium, for the first time.

ETHER
Smelly, sickly and explosive!

What was ether?
Ether was an anaesthetic. *(p.49)*

Why wasn't ether more widely used?
Ether was an effective form of pain relief, but had unpleasant side effects (such as vomiting). It was also highly flammable.

When was ether first successfully used in surgery?
Ether was first used successfully in 1846, in a leg amputation.

Who first used ether successfully?
Robert Liston *(p.49)* first used ether successfully in Britain.

> **DID YOU KNOW?**
>
> **American aristocrats were using ether recreationally at the turn of the century.**
>
> They would hold parties called 'ether frolics'

CHLOROFORM
'That blessed chloroform!'
Queen Victoria

What is chloroform?
Chloroform was an effective form of pain relief.

Who was the first doctor to use chloroform during surgery?
James Simpson *(p.53)*, a professor of midwifery at Edinburgh University, experimented with chloroform on himself and friends.

When did James Simpson discover that chloroform could be used as an anaesthetic?
James Simpson *(p.53)* discovered that chloroform could be used as an anaesthetic *(p.49)* in 1847.

How did James Simpson first use chloroform?
James Simpson *(p.53)* used chloroform on women in childbirth.

Why was there opposition to the use of chloroform?
There were 3 main reasons why some people opposed the use of chloroform.
- ✅ Some army surgeons believed that soldiers should endure pain.
- ✅ Some religious people believed it was God's intention that women should feel pain in childbirth, and that suffering during surgery was God's will.
- ✅ It was difficult to get the dosage right. This was demonstrated when 14-year-old Hannah Greener died while having an ingrown toenail removed.

Who made chloroform more popular?
Chloroform finally became accepted when Queen Victoria used it during the delivery of her eighth child. After this, patients began to ask for it in their operations.

Why was the use of chloroform dangerous?
Chloroform led to the so-called Black Period of surgery, when death rates increased because, with unconscious patients, surgeons were taking their time and doing more advanced surgeries. This meant they were unknowingly taking infection deeper into the body.

How was chloroform use made safer?
John Snow *(p.60)* developed a type of chloroform inhaler and calculated the correct dose per patient, making it much safer and preventing an overdose.

DID YOU KNOW?

After its discovery, chloroform was sometimes used by criminals in robberies, rapes and murders.

HANNAH GREENER
14-year-old dies of chloroform overdose

Who was Hannah Greener?
Hannah Greener was a 14 year old who died while having surgery, an ingrown toenail removal, in 1848 *(p.58)*. in 1848. It is believed she died of an overdose of chloroform *(p.51)* before dosages were known.

COCAINE
A problematic alternative

How was cocaine used in surgery?
Cocaine was used as a local anaesthetic *(p.49)* to numb parts of the body.

When was cocaine used in surgery?
Cocaine was first used as a local anaesthetic *(p.49)* in 1884.

> **DID YOU KNOW?**
>
> In the 19th century, scientists worked out how to extract cocaine from the leaves of the coca tree.

JAMES SIMPSON
The 'Father of Anaesthetics'

Who was James Simpson?
James Simpson was a Scottish doctor in the 1800s who experimented with different types of anaesthetics for use during childbirth. He discovered that chloroform *(p.51)* was effective, and had limited side effects when used in the correct dose.

ANTISEPTICS
Substances to kill the germs

What are antiseptics?
Antiseptics are subtances used to kill microorganisms and prevent infection.

When were antiseptics developed?
Understanding of infection increased during the 1840s with the work of Ignaz Semmelweis. The first antiseptic, carbolic acid *(p.53)*, was used by Joseph Lister *(p.54)* in 1865.

CARBOLIC ACID
An effective antiseptic

What was carbolic acid?
Carbolic acid, or phenol, wasthe first true antiseptic *(p.53)* used in surgery.

How was carbolic acid discovered?
Joseph Lister *(p.54)* studied Pasteur's *(p.43)* germ theory *(p.43)* and, after realising carbolic acid was effective in stopping wounds from turning gangrenous, he developed a carbolic acid spray to kill germs on both medical instruments and the wound.

When was carbolic acid first used?
Joseph Lister *(p.54)* first used carbolic acid, in the form of a spray, in 1865.

How was carbolic acid used in antiseptic surgery.
Antiseptic *(p.53)* surgery involved cleaning surgical instruments, and the patient's wounds, with carbolic acid.

What results did Lister achieve by using carbolic acid?
By using Lister's *(p.54)* antiseptic *(p.53)* techniques, the death rate among patients who had amputations dropped from 46% to 15%.

Why was Lister criticised for his use of carbolic acid?
There were 5 main reasons why there was opposition to Lister's *(p.54)* methods.
- Carbolic acid made the instruments tricky to hold, because they were slippery.
- Carbolic acid was unpleasant to use, as it irritated surgeons' hands.
- Doctors applied Lister's *(p.54)* methods incorrectly, leading them to believe his theory was wrong.
- The equipment was expensive to buy and set up.
- Lister *(p.54)* was arrogant, and disliked by many of the surgical community.

Why did Lister use catgut soaked in carbolic acid?
Lister *(p.54)* used catgut as a ligature. It could be soaked in carbolic acid, which helped prevent infection in the wound.

DID YOU KNOW?

Joseph Lister came up with the idea of carbolic acid because it was used on fields to neutralise the smell of the sewage used as fertiliser.

He realised that it would be safe to use because it didn't hurt the animals that then grazed on the land.

JOSEPH LISTER
The 'Father of Aseptic Surgery'

Who was Joseph Lister?
Joseph Lister was a British surgeon who pioneered the use of antiseptic *(p.53)* techniques in surgery.

ASEPTIC SURGERY
Creating a germ-free environment for surgery

What is aseptic surgery?
Aseptic surgery ensures that operations are carried out in sterile conditions.

What was the difference between antiseptic and aseptic surgery?
Antiseptic *(p.53)* surgery destroys germs on a surgeon's hands, instruments, and immediate surroundings using chemicals e.g. carbolic acid *(p.53)*. Aseptic surgery aims to achieve a completely sterile environment, free from germs, using a combination of measures such as heat and antiseptics.

When was aseptic surgery established?
Aseptic surgery had become common by the year 1900.

What methods were used in aseptic surgery?
There were four key elements to aseptic surgery.
- Surgeons were scrubbed clean before operating. Today, modern surgeons still 'scrub in' before going into theatre.
- Surgeons wore new clothes and a fresh pair of thin rubber gloves for each operation.
- All instruments used during surgery were sterilised beforehand, using steam.
- The size of operating theatres got smaller, to reduce the risk of infection, and spectators were no longer allowed.

> **DID YOU KNOW?**
>
> **Ignaz Semmelweis introduced aseptic procedures in the late 1840s, with great success.**
>
> The death rate on his Viennese maternity ward fell, from 35% to 1%, when he instructed his staff to wash their hands with calcium chloride solution.

INDUSTRIALISATION
Awful living conditions cause problems to health

What was public health like in the mid-nineteenth century?
Industrialisation had a huge negative impact on public health and living conditions. It led to overcrowding and increased the spread of disease.

How did housing conditions affect public health in industrial Britain?
Houses were built cheaply and as close together as possible. They were usually damp, with little light or ventilation.

How did sanitary conditions affect public health in industrial Britain?
There was usually an inadequate supply of clean water, and poor removal of sewage and rubbish. One toilet could be used by 100 people.

> **DID YOU KNOW?**
>
> **Infant mortality was high in industrial towns.**
> In Manchester, in 1842, 57% of all children died before they were five years old.

DISEASE IN INDUSTRIAL CITIES
Lice, poor ventilation and dirty water cause ill-health

What diseases were common in the 1800s?
During the nineteenth century, diseases could spread quickly, particularly in towns and cities. The most common were typhoid, cholera *(p.59)*, tuberculosis, and typhus.

Why did disease spread easily in the mid 19th century?
Living conditions in industrial towns and cities were poor, so diseases could spread easily and quickly.

What was typhoid in industrial Britain?
Typhoid was spread via contaminated food and water. Symptoms included headaches and fever.

What was cholera disease in industrial Britain?
Cholera *(p.59)* was spread through contaminated food and water. Symptoms involved extreme vomiting and diarrhoea.

What was tuberculosis in industrial Britain?
Tuberculosis affected the lungs and was spread by infected people sneezing and coughing. It was also more common in badly-ventilated and damp houses. Symptoms included coughing up blood and weight loss.

What was typhus in in the 1850s?
Typhus was spread through body lice. Symptoms included fever and headaches.

> **DID YOU KNOW?**
>
> **The food available in nineteenth century towns was often impure.**
> It was common for milk to be watered down with chalk, and for butter to be coloured with copper.

EDWIN CHADWICK

A civil servant reports on public health

Who was Edwin Chadwick?

Edwin Chadwick was a civil servant who was involved with the workhouses. He was asked by the government to report on the living conditions and health of the poor.

What was Chadwick's report called?

Chadwick's report, called 'Report on the Sanitary *(p.58)* Conditions of the Labouring Population', was published in 1842.

What conclusions did Chadwick claim in his report?

Edwin Chadwick's report reached 4 main conclusions:

- ☑ Ill-health was caused by the awful conditions in which people lived.
- ☑ If towns were cleaner, there wouldn't be as much disease, and people would not have to take time off work. This would result in fewer people needing the workhouses, which would save ratepayers money.
- ☑ Clean water and sewage disposal was needed for a healthy nation.

Why did Chadwick suggest people could save money by looking after the poor?

Local governments should be responsible for public health and set up boards of health. People would pay taxes to pay for this; but it would save money in the long term, as living conditions improved and fewer people used workhouses.

What did Chadwick recommend to improve health?

Chadwick made two recommendations to address poor living conditions as a cause of disease.

- ☑ A drainage system and refuse collections should be organised.
- ☑ A medical officer should be appointed to each area.

How did the government react to Chadwick's proposals?

Chadwick's ideas about increasing rates were not popular. It was not until there was a further cholera *(p.59)* epidemic that the government began to act on his recommendations.

DID YOU KNOW?

Politicians and civil servants who agreed with the Chadwick's ideas, and wanted better public health, were known as the 'Clean Party'.

The group of politicians and civil servants who believed that health was not the government's responsibility were known as the 'Dirty Party'.

FIRST PUBLIC HEALTH ACT

Encouraging towns to improve public health

What was the Public Health Act of 1848?
The 1848 Public Health Act was the first attempt by the government to enforce the clean up of towns in England and Wales.

What did the Public Health Act 1848 recommend?
The 1848 Public Health Act made four main recommendations.
- Each town could appoint a Medical Officer of Health.
- A general Board of Health could be set up, and towns would be allowed to create their own local boards of health.
- Rubbish removals could be organised, and a sewer system built.
- People should have access to clean water.

What were the problems with the Public Health Act of 1848?
The Public Health Act had of 1848 had limited impact. There were two main reasons for this.
- The terms of the Act were only temporary.
- The Act was voluntary. To create a local board of health required 10% of ratepayers to be in favour, and some local authorities did not take action.

What was the significance of the Public Health Act 1848?
This was the first time the government had passed a law to improve public health, and demonstrates the move away from a laissez-faire *(p.40)* attitude.

DID YOU KNOW?

By 1872, only 50 towns had a medical officer.

SANITARY ACT

Appointing inspectors

What was the Sanitary Act of 1866?
The Sanitary Act of 1866 required towns to appoint inspectors to check on water supplies and drainage.

CHOLERA
The 'Blue Death'

What is cholera?
Cholera is a potentially deadly disease that causes severe sickness, diarrhoea and dehydration.

What was cholera's nickname?
Cholera was nicknamed 'the blue death' as it ruptured blood vessels, and skin turned blue as people became dehydrated.

When were there outbreaks of cholera?
Cholera first arrived in Britain in 1831. There were further outbreaks in 1848 *(p.58)*, 1853, and 1865.

How many people died in each outbreak of cholera?
The number of deaths varied in each outbreak:
- In 1831-32, London suffered 5,275 deaths. In total, the outbreak killed 21,882 across Britain.
- In 1848 *(p.58)*-49, 53,292 people died.
- In 1853-54, 20,097 people died.
- In 1865-66, 14,378 people died.

Who discovered the causes for cholera?
A doctor called John Snow *(p.60)*.

How did John Snow discover the cause of cholera?
Snow *(p.60)* studied deaths from cholera and made a map of them. He traced the source of the outbreak to a water pump on Broad Street, London.

When was the cause of cholera discovered?
The cause of cholera was discovered in 1854.

What did John Snow think about the causes of cholera?
As many of the victims of the 1854 outbreak lived near a water pump on Broad Street, Snow *(p.60)* theorised that cholera could not be caused by miasma and was instead spread by contaminated water.

What was done to prevent the spread of cholera?
The government had a laissez-faire *(p.40)* attitude, which meant that they stayed out of public health issues. As a result, people tried 2 main ways to prevent cholera:
- Many thought it was caused by miasma, so tried to prevent it by cleaning up dirty streets.
- In 1848 *(p.58)*, the first Public Health Act suggested that towns and cities provide clean water supplies. However, as it was not compulsory, its impact was limited.

Why was there opposition to John Snow's discovery of the cause of cholera?
Some doctors disagreed with Snow's *(p.60)* findings. Pasteur's *(p.43)* germ theory *(p.43)* had not been published so Snow's idea that cholera was transmitted through contaminated water, rather than through miasma could not be proven.

Get our free app at GCSEHistory.com

How was the cholera outbreak of 1854 ended?
Snow *(p.60)* asked for the handle of the Broad Street water pump to be removed, so people could not use it. The outbreak quickly ended, proving the disease had come from the water in the pump. It was later found that a cesspit had been leaking into the well.

 Why were Snow's cholera findings important?
John Snow *(p.60)* had 2 main impacts.
- ✅ In 1855, he presented the results of his investigation to Parliament, and suggested that a new sewer system was built, something the government later agreed to.
- ✅ Snow *(p.60)* proved that cholera was not carried through the air like a poisonous gas *(p.93)* or miasma.

> **DID YOU KNOW?**
> A cholera victim could expel up to 20 litres of diarrhoea.

JOHN SNOW
The 'Father of Modern Epidemiology'

 Who was John Snow?
John Snow was the doctor responsible for discovering that cholera *(p.59)* was a water-borne disease.

 What else did John Snow discover?
John Snow also invented an inhaler that could be used to administer chloroform *(p.51)* safely by controlling the dose.

> **DID YOU KNOW?**
> **John Snow was the doctor responsible for Queen Victoria using chloroform during the birth of her eighth child.**
> After this, Victoria referred to it as 'that blessed chloroform!'. This contributed to the public acceptance of the use of the anaesthetic.

THE GREAT STINK
The filthy River Thames becomes impossible to ignore

 What was the Great Stink?
A heatwave in the summer of 1858 caused the River Thames to smell much worse than it usually did, due to the evaporation of water. As a result, the river had a more concentrated sewage content.

How did Parliament react to the Great Stink?

The smell was so bad that politicians in the Houses of Parliament, next to the river, demanded to meet somewhere else. MPs asked for help from Joseph Bazalgette *(p.61)*, a civil engineer.

What was the significance of the Great Stink?

The Great Stink of 1858 had 2 main effects.
- ☑ The sewer system beneath London was built, which greatly improved conditions in the city.
- ☑ The Great Stink marked the end of the laissez-faire *(p.40)* attitude of government.

DID YOU KNOW?

Temperatures during the summer of 1858 reached over 30 degrees celsius.

JOSEPH BAZALGETTE
Master engineer builds the London sewers

Who was Joseph Bazalgette?

Joseph Bazalgette was a civil engineer in the 1800s.

What was Bazalgette's contribution to public health?

He was the chief designer and engineer on London's sewer system, ordered after the Great Stink *(p.60)*.

What was Bazalgette's sewer system like?

It was designed to remove waste from London's streets by carrying waste downriver towards the sea. The main sewers covered a distance of 83 miles and removed 420 million gallons of sewage per day.

When was Bazalgette's sewer system built?

The system was offically opened in 1865, although the systme continued to be developed into the 1870s.

How much did Bazalgette's sewer system cost?

The system cost £3 million.

DID YOU KNOW?

Bazalgette's sewers used 318 million bricks!
There were a total of about 1,300 miles of sewers and drains built under London.

SECOND PUBLIC HEALTH ACT

Forcing towns to improve public health

What was the Public Health Act of 1875?
The second Public Health Act of 1875 was the government's attempt to enforce action to reduce some public health-related illnesses and diseases, such as cholera *(p.59)*.

Why did the government pass the Public Health Act 1875?
The second Public Health Act of 1875 was passed as the government began to realise that public health was part of their responsibility.

What measures were in the 1875 Public Health Act?
The Public Health Act of 1875 made local authorities responsible for 3 main areas of public health measures.
- ✅ There must be provision of clean water and proper disposal of rubbish and sewage.
- ✅ Medical Officers of Health should be appointed in every area.
- ✅ There were standards for new housing, and lodging houses should be checked.

Why was the 1875 Public Health Act an improvement on the 1848 Public Health Act?
The 1875 Health Act was different from the 1848 *(p.58)* Health Act because it was compulsory - local authorities were forced to carry out the improvements.

Why was the 1875 Public Health Act significant?
The second act signified a change in the government's laissez-faire *(p.40)* attitude. Laws were now being passed to improve public health and they had to be obeyed.

> **DID YOU KNOW?**
>
> **In 1867 Manchester led the country in toilets.**
>
> The local authorities abolished midden privies (a toilet over a pit) and replaced them with pail privies. These were much easier to empty and clean.

BLOOD GROUPS

Solving the problem of blood-loss

What are blood transfusions?
Blood transfusions are when blood from another person is introduced into a patient's body.

When was the first blood transfusion?
The first blood transfusion was carried out in 1818.

Who discovered blood transfusion?
James Blundell *(p.49)* carried out early blood transfusions, publishing his paper 'Experiments on the Transfusion of Blood by the Syringe' in 1818.

How were blood transfusions performed before the twentieth century?
Because blood clotted when it was removed from the body, early blood transfusions were directly donor-to-patient, and the donor had to be present.

Why were blood transfusions unsuccessful before 1901?
Only 50% of transfusions were successful before 1901.. There were 3 key problems:
- As blood could not be stored, transfusions involved the donor being directly attached to the recipient by a tube.
- It could often lead to death through infection.
- Patients' bodies rejected the new blood because they were given the wrong blood type, as blood groups had yet to be discovered.

How did the discovery of blood groups help in transfusions?
There were 3 key discoveries that led to more successful blood transfusions.
- In 1901, Karl Landsteiner *(p.63)* discovered the A, B and O blood groups.
- In 1902, he discovered another blood group, AB.
- In 1907, it was discovered that type O blood was 'universal' and could safely be given to anyone.

What was the impact of blood transfusions?
Successful and safe blood transfusions helped with medical treatments in 3 main ways.
- They could be used in surgery.
- They could help patients suffering from blood disorders such as anaemia or leukaemia.
- They could be used to help people with liver problems, such as jaundice.

DID YOU KNOW?

In the 17th century, surgeons experimented with blood transfusions between sheep and people.
This had an enormously high death rate, but apparently a few people survived!

KARL LANDSTEINER
The 'Father of Transfusion Medicine'

Who was Karl Landsteiner?
Karl Landsteiner was an Austrian scientist who discovered different blood groups, making transfusions safer.

MAGIC BULLETS
Targetting the germs that cause disease

What is a magic bullet?
A magic bullet is a chemical compound that will kill a specific germ without harming other cells.

Who discovered the magic bullet?
Paul Ehrlich *(p.65)* worked with Robert Koch *(p.45)*, Emil von Behring *(p.76)* and Sahachiro Hata *(p.66)*. He is known for discovering the first 'magic bullet'.

How did Paul Ehrlich discover the first magic bullet?
There were 2 main stages in Ehrlich's *(p.65)* discovery of magic bullets.
- In 1900, he suggested some chemicals might be able to kill specific germs.
- In 1909, Paul Ehrlich *(p.65)* and Sahachiro Hata *(p.66)* discovered the compound Salvarsan 606, which could kill the syphilis germ.

What was the first magic bullet?
The first magic bullet was Salvarsan 606, which was the 606th chemical compound tested by Ehrlich's *(p.65)* team to treat syphilis.

What was the impact of the discovery of magic bullets?
Magic bullets had 3 key impacts on medicine.
- The discovery of magic bullets marked the birth of the modern pharmaceutical industry.
- In 1932, Gerhard Domagk *(p.66)* discovered that blood poisoning could be cured using Prontosil *(p.65)*.
- In 1935, French and Italian scientists at the Pasteur *(p.43)* Institute in Paris discovered bacteriostatic antibiotics based on how Prontosil *(p.65)* affected the body. They had realised that bacteria in the body could not multiply because of Prontosil.

When were magic bullets developed?
The development of magic bullets took a number of years.
- The idea of magic bullets was first suggested by Paul Ehrlich *(p.65)* in 1900.
- Salvarsan 606, the first magic bullet, was discovered in 1909.

DID YOU KNOW?

As well as discovering the cure for syphilis, Paul Ehrlich made a number of other significant medical discoveries.
He also made medical breakthroughs in haematology, chemotherapy and immunology.

PRONTOSIL
A red dye becomes a cure

What was Prontosil?
Prontosil is a chemical used to make a red dye that contains sulphonamide. It was found to be the 'magic bullet *(p.64)*' that killed the streptococcus infection.

When was Prontosil discovered?
Gerhard Domagk *(p.66)* discovered Prontosil could kill streptococcus in 1932.

How did Domagk test Prontosil?
In 1935, Gerhard Domagk *(p.66)* used Prontosil to cure his daughter of infection.

Who discovered Prontosil?
Gerhard Domagk *(p.66)* was a German scientist who discovered that Prontosil could be used as a magic bullet *(p.64)* against bacteria that caused infection.

What was Prontosil used for?
The discovery of Prontosil's magic bullet *(p.64)* properties was useful in 2 main ways.
- It was found to be effective in curing puerperal fever in new mothers.
- The main ingredient, sulphonamide, was developed to treat pneumonia, scarlet fever and meningitis.

> **DID YOU KNOW?**
>
> **Domagk used prontosil to save the life of his daughter.**
> When she was six years old, Hildegard Domagk contracted a streptococcal infection from an unsterilised needle. Although the prontosil cured her, it gave her skin a permanent reddish tinge.

PAUL EHRLICH
The doctor who discovered Prontosil

Who was Paul Ehrlich?
Paul Ehrlich was German scientist and physician. He studied blood and immunology, and discovered the cure for syphilis, Salvarsan 606. He was awarded a Nobel Prize in 1908.

SAHACHIRO HATA
Part of the team who discovered the magic bullet

Who was Sahachiro Hata?
Sahachiro Hata is known for being part of the team that discovered the first 'magic bullet *(p.64)*'.

GERHARD DOMAGK
German pathologist and bacteriologist.

Who was Gerhard Domagk?
Gerhard Domagk was a German scientist who discovered that Prontosil *(p.65)* could be used as a magic bullet *(p.64)* against bacteria that caused infection.

ALEXANDER FLEMING
Discovering penicillin

Who was Alexander Fleming?
Sir Alexander Fleming was a Scottish scientist, who discovered the antibiotic *(p.67)* properties of penicillin in 1928.

What was Alexander Fleming's background?
Alexander Fleming had been an army doctor *(p.95)* in the First World War *(p.82)*, where he saw many men die of infection caused by the staphylococcus bacteria and septicaemia.

What were Fleming's early discoveries?
In 1922, Fleming's research identified that an enzyme called lysozyme, found in human tears, killed certain harmless bacteria.

How did Fleming discover penicillin?
In 1928, Fleming accidentally left some staphylococcus bacteria on a culture plate in his lab. After two weeks he noticed that penicillium notatum (a green *(p.52)* mould) had stopped the bacteria from growing.

Where did Fleming publish his findings?
In 1929, Fleming published his findings about penicillin *(p.67)* in the 'British Journal of Experimental Pathology'.

What problems did Fleming face?
Fleming was unable to develop his research into penicillin *(p.67)* after 1929 for 3 key reasons:
- ☑ It was difficult to grow enough penicillium (the fungus) for effective research.
- ☑ Penicillin *(p.67)* appeared to take time to have an effect, and its effectiveness was limited when mixed with blood.
- ☑ Fleming was unable to get funding for more research.

> **DID YOU KNOW?**
>
> **Fleming studied a wide range of sciences.**
> He was a biologist, physician, microbiologist and pharmacologist.

PENICILLIN AND ANTIBIOTICS
Developing the use of antibiotics

What is penicillin?
Penicillin was the first antibiotic to be discovered, and was originally derived from common penicillium mould.

What type of medicine is penicillin?
Antibiotics are microbes that can kill the germs that cause diseases.

How did people use penicillin before it was discovered?
In the Middle Ages, people used mouldy bread to treat infection in a wound, and in 1871 Joseph Lister (p.54) used it to treat a patient.

When was penicillin discovered?
Penicillin was discovered in 1928.

What bacteria did penicillin treat?
The staphylococcus bacteria is a germ that causes many infections.

Who developed Fleming's research on penicillin?
In 1939, Howard Florey (p.68) and Ernst Chain (p.69) at Oxford University began to look into Fleming's (p.66) discoveries. Helped by Norman Heatley, they conducted more tests.

How did Florey and Chain test penicillin?
Florey (p.68) and Chain (p.69) tested penicillin in 3 stages although they found it difficult to produce enough to be effective:

- In 1940, their first tests were on mice, which recovered from streptococci with penicillin.
- In 1941, their first human subject was a policeman with septicaemia. The penicillin helped, but there was not enough to cure him and he died.
- They developed penicillin to treat children, as a smaller dose was needed.

Who funded the development of penicillin?
Americans were initially responsible for funding the large-scale production of penicillin. Florey (p.68) travelled to the U.S. to seek help from the American pharmaceutical industry. They convinced four drug companies to invest.

Why was it possible to mass-produce penicillin?

Penicillin could be mass-produced for 5 key reasons:

- ✅ Individuals such as Fleming *(p.66)*, Florey *(p.68)* and Chain *(p.69)* were actively looking for solutions to infections. Florey's decision not to patent their findings made penicillin affordable.
- ✅ The development of techniques to grow and observe germs helped scientists discover antibiotics.
- ✅ The First World War *(p.82)* showed the impact that infections could have in wartime, while the Second World War gave governments the incentive to find and fund solutions.
- ✅ The technological advance of mass production techniques made it easier to make penicillin.
- ✅ The American government funded Florey's *(p.68)* research for five years. Institutions such as governments funded and encouraged the production of penicillin.

What is the impact of penicillin?

Penicillin is estimated to have saved 200 million lives since its development.

How has penicillin been developed further?

A synthetic (chemical) version of penicillin was created in 1955.

Who got the Nobel Prize for penicillin?

In 1945, Fleming *(p.66)*, Florey *(p.68)* and Chain *(p.69)* were jointly awarded the Nobel Prize for Medicine for their work on penicillin.

Why are scientists constantly researching new antibiotics?

Scientists are constantly working on researching and finding new antibiotics. This is because of the problem of the development of penicillin-resistant bacteria.

DID YOU KNOW?

In the early stages of their research, Florey and Chain struggled to grow enough penicillin to treat a human.

Because there was so little penicillin in the mould, they grew mould on as many available surfaces as they could - including milk bottles, tea trays and bedpans. Later, Americans would use gigantic beer vats to produce the mould.

HOWARD FLOREY

Australian pathologist who developed research into penicillin

Who was Howard Florey?

Howard Florey was an Australian scientist who worked with Ernst Chain *(p.69)* to further research the potential of penicillin *(p.67)*.

ERNST CHAIN
German biochemist who developed research into penicillin

Who was Ernst Chain?
Ernst Chain was a German scientist who worked with Howard Florey *(p.68)* to develop tests on penicillin *(p.67)*.

RADIATION
Used as a treatment for cancer.

What is radiation?
Radiation is the emission or transmission of energy through space or through material, which takes place in the form of waves or particles. These particles can be used to treat certain diseases and illnesses.

MARIE CURIE
Scientist who investigated radiation.

Who was Marie Curie?
Marie Curie was a Polish chemist who was awarded a Nobel Prize in 1903. She worked on radioactive elements, and died of radiation *(p.69)* exposure.

What discoveries did Marie Curie make?
Marie Curie made 2 important discoveries.
- ✅ She found two new radioactive elements, polonium and radium, in 1898.
- ✅ She discovered that radiation *(p.69)* could be used to shrink tumours.

What did Marie Curie do in the First World War?
Marie Curie was involved in 2 main activities during the First World War *(p.82)*:
- ✅ She put her research into a bank, and spent the First World War *(p.82)* building mobile X-rays in cars and portable X-rays for base hospitals.
- ✅ She trained over 150 female friends and volunteers on how to drive and use the X-rays. They then drove these radiological cars, known as 'little Curies', around the Western Front to help the war effort.

DID YOU KNOW?

During the First World War, Marie Curie donated twenty mobile X-ray units to the French army.

These were known as 'petite Curies' (little Curies).

X-RAYS
A way to see inside the body.

How do x-rays work?
X-rays work by passing radiation *(p.69)* through the body to produce images of bones, organs and tissue.

Who invented the X-ray machine?
The X-ray machine was invented by a German physicist named Wilhelm Roentgen *(p.70)*.

When was the X-ray machine invented?
The X-ray machine was invented in 1895. The X-ray machine was very quickly put to use and was being used in London hospitals by 1896.

How could X-rays assist in medical treatment?
X-ray machines helped doctors in 4 key ways:

- They could show broken bones so they could be set properly.
- They could show where bullets or other foreign objects were lodged in the body.
- They could be used to identify the shadow on a lung that indicated tuberculosis.
- They could be used to show internal organs if the patient swallowed something that showed up on the X-ray.

> **DID YOU KNOW?**
>
> **Doctors were quick to obtain and experiment with X-ray machines.**
>
> John MacIntrye, at Glasgow Royal Infirmary, produced X-rays of a penny in a child's throat and a frog kicking its legs.

WILHELM ROENTGEN
The scientist who discovered X-rays

Who was Wilhelm Roentgen?
Wilhelm Roentgen was a German physicist, who first discovered that radiation *(p.69)* could be used to produce an image of bones inside the body. He invented a machine that became known as the X-ray *(p.70)* machine.

GENETIC UNDERSTANDING
Building blocks of life

What is DNA?
DNA carries the information needed to develop the characteristics of any living organism. It is the building block of human cells and is responsible for passing on genetic characteristics to children.

Where was DNA discovered?
DNA was discovered at Cambridge University.

What does DNA stand for?
DNA stands for Deoxyribonucleic Acid.

How was DNA discovered?
DNA had already been discovered by scientists in the late 1800s, but in 1963 scientists James Watson *(p.72)* and Francis Crick *(p.72)* discovered its double helix structure which allowed later scientists to understand genetic diseases.

How did scientists learn about DNA?
The Human Genome Project *(p.71)* was set up in 1990 to better understand human DNA. Teams of scientists mapped all the genes in DNA to understand the effect each one had on the body.

DID YOU KNOW?

If unwound and linked together, the strands of DNA in a single human cell would be six feet long.

The DNA from all the cells in a human body would stretch from the earth to the sun!

THE HUMAN GENOME PROJECT
A worldwide research project

What was the Human Genome Project?
The Human Genome Project involved an international team of scientists working together to decode the human genome. As a result of their efforts, there is now a 'genetic blueprint' for human beings.

When was the Human Genome Project?
The Human Genome Project lasted from 1990 to 2003. It finished two years ahead of schedule.

Who set up the Human Genome Project?
James Watson *(p.72)* set up the Human Genome Project.

How has the Human Genome Project been used to treat illness and disease?

Once DNA *(p.71)* had been mapped, scientists could use the information to treat people suffering from genetic diseases. Examples include:

- ☑ A gene was identified that is sometimes present in breast cancer sufferers. People can now be tested to see whether they carry that gene.
- ☑ It has been used to reverse mutations that cause blindness.
- ☑ It has been used to make some cells resistant to HIV (the virus that causes AIDS).

JAMES WATSON

Watson is an American geneticist and biophysicist who played a crucial role in the discovery of the molecular structure of DNA

Who was James Watson?

James Watson was an American biologist at Cambridge University. He worked on discovering and understanding DNA *(p.71)*, and won a Nobel Prize.

FRANCIS CRICK

Crick is a British scientist best known for his work with James Watson which led to the identification of the structure of DNA in 1953

Who was Francis Crick?

Francis Crick was an English physicist at Cambridge University. He worked on discovering and understanding DNA *(p.71)*, and won a Nobel Prize.

ROSALIND FRANKLIN

Franklin is best known for her work on the X-ray diffraction images of DNA, particularly Photo 51, while at King's College London, which led to the discovery of the DNA double helix

Who was Rosalind Franklin?

Rosalind Franklin was an English chemist and X-ray *(p.70)* crystallographer at King's College, London. She worked on discovering DNA *(p.71)*, and was the only member of the team not to be awarded a Nobel Prize.

MAURICE WILKINS

Wilkins initiated the experimental research into DNA that culminated in Watson and Crick's discovery of its structure in 1953.

Who was Maurice Wilkins?

Maurice Wilkins was a physicist and molecular biologist at King's College London. He worked on the discovery of DNA *(p.71)*, and won a Nobel Prize.

NEW TECHNOLOGY IN THE 20TH CENTURY

Computers, lasers, sound-waves, robots...

What is new technology used for in the development of medicine?

As technology advances in the modern world there is now a wide range of machines and technologies used to diagnose, monitor and treat patients.

What are the different types of new technology in medicine used for?

New technology is used in a variety of ways in modern medicine.

- Various monitors can be used to check a patient's blood pressure, oxygen levels, and heart rate.
- During the 1990s, increased use of keyhole surgery - using endoscopes - allowed surgeons to carry out complex surgery with minimal trauma to patients and a reduced risk of infection. This can now be done using robotics, making incisions even smaller.
- MRI scanning and CT scanning create 3D images of the skeleton and soft tissue inside the body. This helps doctors diagnose and treat patients more accurately.
- In-vitro fertilisation, or IVF, was discovered in the 1970s as a way to help those with fertility issues have children.
- Dialysis machines are used to treat the blood of patients with kidney failure.
- Prosthetic limbs are used to replace lost body parts: for example, for soldiers in war.
- Lasers and robotics can be used for precision in surgery.
- Surgeons now have the ability to transplant organs through surgery. The first kidney was transplanted in 1956, between identical twins. The first lungs were transplanted in 1963, and the first heart in 1967.

DID YOU KNOW?

Robots are being used more and more in medicine!

Robots have been used more and more in medicine to do routine operations, as well as performing operations in hard-to-reach places.

ALTERNATIVE MEDICINE
Unconventional methods of tackling health problems

What is alternative medicine?
Alternative medicine is any other way of treating an illness that doesn't rely on scientific, peer-reviewed, proven and doctor-dispensed medicine.

Why do people use alternative medicines?
People use this because there are still no cures for certain syndromes such as AIDS or some types of cancer so they turn to alternative ways of improving their health.

How does alternative medicine work?
Many alternative treatments are intended to consider the patient as a whole, instead of using mainstream medicines to target a specific problem or part of the body.

How popular is alternative medicine?
Since the 1980s, alternative treatments have become popular. Approximately, 1 in 5 people in Britain have used alternative medicines.

How are prevention methods used as alternative medicine?
There has been more focus on preventing illnesses rather than curing them. This is done through living healthy lifestyles, regularly exercising, and avoiding sugary, fatty foods.

What are some examples of alternative medicines?
There are four examples of alternative medicines used in Britain.
- [x] Aromatherapy.
- [x] Acupuncture.
- [x] Hypnotherapy.
- [x] Homeopathy.

Why do some people oppose alternative treatments?
People oppose alternative treatments for different reasons:
- [x] There is a lack of regulation. Anyone is able to practise alternative medicine without formal qualifications.
- [x] There is a lack of scientfic proof that it works. Doctors in particular often dismiss it as 'quackery'.

DID YOU KNOW?

The global market for alternative medicine was estimated to be worth $69.2 billion in 2019.

PREVENTION
Vaccination, public health and campaigns

How do people prevent disease in the modern day?

The government has taken a much larger role in public health and the prevention of disease since the 1900s, especially after the establishment of the NHS *(p.81)* in 1948.

What types of prevention were used in the 20th century?

There are different ways in which the government and people prevent disease in the modern day, these are:

- Compulsory vaccinations: the government have introduced several compulsory vaccinations, for example diphtheria *(p.76)*, measles, and rubella.
- Laws that help to provide a healthy environment for us to live in: for example, the Clean Air Acts, and rules surrounding clean water and good housing.
- Lifestyle campaigns: the government has launched several campaigns to help people make healthier choices, for example Change4Life, and anti-smoking campaigns.
- Quarantine measures: During the 2013-16 Ebola outbreak in West Africa, the government implemented quarantine measures for travellers from the areas of outbreak to protect the country and prevent a global outbreak.
- Charities also try to help through campaigns, research and support: for example, the British Heart Foundation.

What vaccinations were introduced for prevention in the 20th century?

The government introduced several national vaccination campaigns. However, a small number of people do not trust vaccinations and choose not to use them.

- In 1942, a national vaccination campaign was introduced to combat diphtheria. *(p.76)*
- A vaccination for polio *(p.77)* (poliomyelitis) was introduced in the 1950s.
- Other vaccinations that have been introduced include: whooping cough in 1950, tetanus in 1961, measles in 1968, and rubella in 1970.
- The most recent example is the HPV vaccination given in schools, to prevent infection from a sexually transmitted disease that can lead to cervical cancer. At first it was only given to girls, but this has been expanded to boys in recent years.
- Each year a flu vaccine is introduced. Although it does not cover all flus it can help protect the most vulnerable from the most common types.

What laws were introduced for prevention in the 20th century?

The government has passed many laws that help to keep our environment safe and healthy. A good example of this is the Clean Air Acts, passed in 1956 and 1968, to reduce smog and pollution.

What campaigns were introduced for prevention in the 20th and 21st centuries?

The government and charities use public campaigns to help inform people of risks to their health and advice on making healthy choices. Examples include:

- Advertising: campaigns have included those on the dangers of smoking, binge drinking, salt, sugar, unprotected sex, and drug use.
- Initiatives: healthy eating has been encouraged through initiatives such as Change4Life.
- Events: Stoptober and other events have been used to support and encourage people to stop smoking.

DID YOU KNOW?

Vaccinations are estimated to prevent 2.5 million deaths a year.

DIPHTHERIA
Tackling a childhood killer

What is diphtheria?
Diphtheria is a serious infection. It can affect the lungs and heart, and can cause paralysis. It can also lead to death, especially in children.

How many people died of diphtheria?
Before the vaccination campaign, around 3,000 children died of diphtheria each year.

When was a vaccination introduced for diphtheria?
A vaccination for diphtheria was introduced in 1942, with the first nationally government funded campaign to encourage vaccinations.

Why was the vaccination for diphtheria introduced?
Due to crowding in air raid shelters during the Second World War, the government was worried that more children would catch and then die of diphtheria.

What was the result of the campaign for diphtheria?
Once the vaccination was introduced the number of cases of diphtheria reduced dramatically. Within a decade the disease was becoming very rare.

> **DID YOU KNOW?**
>
> **Diphtheria has a 10% death rate.**
> The symptoms include a headache, fever and swollen glands. The bacteria then forms a greyish skin on the back of the throat.

EMIL VON BEHRING
Discovering antitoxins to treat diphtheria

Who was Emil von Behring?
Emil von Behring was the scientist who discovered that antitoxins could be used to successfully treat diphtheria. *(p.76)*

When did Emil von Behring discover antitoxins?
Emil von Behring discovered antitoxins in 1890.

> **DID YOU KNOW?**
>
> Emil von Behring was awarded the Nobel Prize in 1901.

POLIO
Another serious disease is nearly eradicated

What is polio?
Polio, also called poliomyelitis, is an infectious disease that causes muscle weakness. It can result in long term disability.

How many cases of polio were there?
By the 1950s, about 8,000 cases of polio were reported in Britain each year.

When was a vaccination introduced for polio?
Jonas Salk *(p.77)* developed a vaccination for polio in the US. In 1956, it was introduced into Britain.

What was the result of the polio vaccination?
Due to the introduction of the vaccination for polio, the last known case of polio in Britain was reported in 1984.

DID YOU KNOW?
0.5% of polio cases lead to irreversible paralysis.

JONAS SALK
US doctor

Who was Jonas Salk?
Jonas Salk developed a vaccination for polio *(p.77)* in the US. In 1956, it was introduced into Britain.

LUNG CANCER
Smoking leads to a deadly disease

What is the impact of lung cancer?
Lung cancer causes the most cancer deaths. It is the second most common cancer in the UK. The peak of deaths from lung cancer happened in 1973, with 26,000 deaths in that year alone.

Does smoking cause lung cancer?
The British Medical Research Council published important research in 1950, which showed a direct link between smoking and lung cancer. However, it was a while before the government acted to discourage smoking.

How much does lung cancer cost the NHS?
According to the government's own figures, each lung cancer patient costs the NHS *(p.81)* more than £9,000 a year. The disease, which is mostly caused by smoking, costs far more to treat than any other cancer and has a devastating impact on the wider economy as well as a stark human cost.

What are the problems with diagnosing lung cancer?
Lung cancer can be hard to detect. People are often diagnosed late, as patients think their symptoms are something else or not serious.

How do we diagnose lung cancer?
Improvements have been made to diagnosis and there is now a specific process to diagnose lung cancer:
- CT scans work to give a detailed image about the inside of the body.
- Patients are injected with a non-toxic dye that makes the lungs show up on the scan.
- A PET-CT may be used in less advanced cases, along with a radioactive dye. Together, they are used to identify cancerous cells.
- In advanced cases, bronchoscopes are put into the lungs to collect a tissue sample for testing.

How do we treat lung cancer?
There are many treatments available, due to modern medicine and technology.
- Part or all of the lung can be removed.
- Lung transplants can be carried out.
- Chemotherapy.
- Radiotherapy.
- Scientists are researching how genetics might be used to treat lung cancer. Genetics might be able to show which treatments would be more effective for the individual.

How does the government try to prevent lung cancer?
The government has taken steps to reduce the number of lung cancer cases in the UK, by highlighting preventative measures people can take.
- In 1965, cigarette advertising on TV was banned.
- In 2005, cigarette advertising was completely banned.
- In 2007, smoking was banned in all enclosed public places and workplaces.
- In 2007, the legal smoking age was raised from 16 to 18.
- In 2012, cigarette packets were removed from display in shops.
- In 2015, smoking in cars carrying children was banned.
- The dangers of smoking are now taught in schools. Shops are not allowed to have tobacco products on display.

How has lung cancer spurred increased government intervention?
Measures have included laws that protect workers from being exposed to cancer-causing substances, such as asbestos, arsenic, nickel, and chromium. Additional laws prevent smoking in the workplace to lower the risk of lung cancer caused by secondhand smoke.

> **DID YOU KNOW?**
>
> **Unlike other types of cancer, there is no national screening programme for lung cancer.**
>
> There has been little evidence that screening helps to prevent lung cancer. The tests that can be done, such as CT scans, could possibly damage the lungs and are also costly.

WELFARE STATE
'From the cradle to the grave'.

What was the purpose of the Welfare State?
After the Second World War, British Prime Minister Clement Attlee and his Labour government set up the welfare state to provide care for everyone, 'from the cradle to the grave'.

How did the Second World War contribute to the creation of the Welfare State?
The Second World War helped to bring about the creation of the Welfare State in 3 key ways.
- The war forced Britain to deal with large numbers of injuries.
- The war expanded the role of the government in health, with the Emergency Medical Service.
- People were shocked at the state of the hygiene and health of some of the evacuees.

What new measures did the Labour government introduce under the Welfare State?
The Labour government introduced 3 main reforms after 1945 that affected health.
- The New Towns Act of 1946 was introduced, to plan new towns.
- The National Insurance Act of 1946 provided better unemployment and sick pay, maternity benefits, and improved old age pensions.
- The National Health Service *(p.81)* was launched in 1948, which provided free healthcare at the point of delivery and was paid for by taxes.

> **DID YOU KNOW?**
>
> **The Welfare State was mostly supported. However, some people objected to it.**
>
> The Welfare State was opposed by some groups of people. Some were afraid that taxes would increase and some believed that it would discourage people from looking for jobs. They feared that people might 'live off the state'.

WILLIAM BEVERIDGE
Liberal politician and social reformer

Who was William Beveridge?
William Beveridge was a government minister, who wrote a report about rebuilding Britain after the Second World War.

When was the Beveridge Report published?
William Beveridge published The Beveridge Report in 1942.

What problems in society did Beveridge suggest the government should tackle?
The Beveridge Report suggested the government had a role to play in tackling the 5 'giant evils' of British society:
- Want (poverty).
- Disease.
- Ignorance (lack of education).
- Squalor (unhygienic living conditions).
- Idleness (unemployment).

What was the significance of the Beveridge Report?
The Beveridge Report became very famous, and raised people's hopes that the government would do more to build a healthier society after the Second World War. It formed the basis of the welfare state. *(p.79)*

How did the governement respond to the Beveridge Report?
The government took 5 key measures to fix the 5 'giant evils'.
- The government introduced a range of benefits. For example a weekly family allowance, paid to the mother.
- The NHS *(p.81)* was created.
- The Clean Air Acts (1952 & 1956) aimed to reduce pollution in towns and cities.
- The government embarked on a slum clearance programme in the 1960s. They were replaced by council housing with modern conveniences such as central heating.
- New towns, such as Milton Keynes, were built from scratch with more space and better public facilities like parks.

DID YOU KNOW?

Beveridge's proposals were popular.
By 1943 around 43% of the British public agreed with the proposals.

ANEURIN BEVAN
'The NHS will last as long as there are folk left with the faith to fight for it'.

Who was Aneurin Bevan?
Aneurin Bevan was a Labour minister from Wales, who was responsible for setting up the NHS *(p.81)* in 1948.

NHS
'Free at the point of delivery'

What was the NHS?
The National Health Service (NHS) was set up to provide free healthcare to patients at the point of delivery.

Who was responsible for establishing the NHS?
Aneurin Bevan *(p.80)* was a Labour Minister for Health from Wales, who was responsible for setting up the NHS.

Why was the NHS introduced?
By the end of the Second World War, changes to society meant that the idea of a public health service was much more popular, for 5 key reasons.
- Many children were evacuated to the country during the Second World War. People were horrified by the poverty that they saw.
- By the mid-twentieth century, people had become more used to the idea of the government playing a role in people's lives.
- Advances in medicine meant that there were more ways to help the sick.
- The Second World War had already forced the government to organise, and take more control of, hospitals and medical services.
- The Beveridge *(p.80)* Report of 1942 inspired the creation of the NHS.

When did the NHS begin?
The NHS was founded on 5th July, 1948.

Who opposed the creation of the NHS?
There were 2 main areas of opposition to the creation of the NHS.
- Some doctors opposed the introduction of the NHS because it reduced their income from private patients. Bevan *(p.80)* promised they could continue to work privately, as well as receiving a salary from the government.
- Many Conservatives disliked the NHS because of the burden on the taxpayer, but it was too popular with the general public to be abolished.

How was the NHS organised?
The NHS was organised in the following ways:
- Hospitals were controlled by 14 regional boards, but were made part of a single system.
- Doctors, as well as dentists, pharmacists and opticians, had individual contracts with the NHS.
- GPs played an important role in providing primary health care, by diagnosing and treating patients, by referring them to hospital where necessary, or writing prescriptions for medicine.
- Local health authorities had responsibility for vaccination programmes, maternal and child welfare, health visitors, and school dental services. They were led by a medical officer.

What services does the NHS provide?
The NHS provides services through medical treatment, hospitals, specialist healthcare professionals, preventative healthcare, and care for the vulnerable.
- The NHS provides treatment for illness and injury, including surgery, blood transfusions and medication.
- The NHS runs hospitals, provides ambulance services to transport *(p.100)* patients to them, and accident and emergency care.

- The NHS provides access to healthcare professionals and services such as GPs, mental health services, dental treatment, and opticians.
- The NHS works to prevent illness to cut down on the cost of treatment. This includes campaigns to encourage healthier lifestyles, vaccinations, and diagnostic screening.
- The NHS provides care for the vulnerable, such as the elderly and disabled. Maternity care and health visitors are provided for mothers and new babies.

 In what ways has the NHS been successful?

The NHS has been successful in improving healthcare in Britain in 6 main ways.

- The NHS has improved hospitals and healthcare facilities.
- The NHS has led to a fall in child mortality rates.
- The NHS has implemented a national vaccination scheme, eradicating many diseases.
- The NHS provides free healthcare for all, regardless of their ability to pay.
- The NHS has raised life expectancy.
- The NHS lowers treatment costs by promoting preventive health care.

 How much did the NHS cost?

The NHS was paid for by National Insurance contributions and taxes. In 1948, it cost £12.9 billion.

 How much did the NHS raise life expectancy?

In 1930, on average, men lived until the age of 58 and women until 62. By 1950, this had increased to 66 for men and 70 for women.

 What happened to the NHS in the 1960s?

During the 1960s, the government built more hospitals across the country, and introduced a GP's charter in 1966, which improved standards in care.

DID YOU KNOW?

The NHS was the first of its kind!

When the NHS was established, on 4th July 1948, it was the first time in history that there had been an organised healthcare system that was based on citizenship rather than having to pay for medical care. Many other countries have used the NHS model for their own healthcare systems.

THE FIRST WORLD WAR CONTEXT

'The war to end all wars'

 How was the First World War fought?

By the end of 1914, both the Allied and German forces had stopped advancing. In order to try to hold the territory they had, each side dug trenches. A new type of warfare had begun.

Which First World War battles were important for medical treatment?

There were many significant locations, events and battles in the First World War. However, some of the most important in the development of medical treatment were:

- First Battle of Ypres (p.84).
- Hill 60 (p.84).
- Second Battle of Ypres (p.85).
- The Somme (p.85).
- Third Battle of Ypres (p.87).
- Arras (p.86).
- Cambrai (p.87).

> **DID YOU KNOW?**
>
> **Studies suggest that only 5.6% of injured soldiers died after receiving medical treatment on the Western Front.**
>
> Of the 2.7 million British casualties, 700,000 died before they could receive medical treatment.

YPRES
A major strategic position on the Western Front

What happened at Ypres?

Ypres is a town in Belgium. There were three major battles there during the war.

When did the Germans attack Ypres?

The 3 main battles occurred throughout the war:

- Germany attacked in October-November 1914 (First Battle of Ypres (p.84)).
- There was a second German attack in April-May 1915 (Second Battle of Ypres (p.85)).
- The British attacked from July to November 1917 (Third Battle of Ypres (p.87), or Passchendaele).

What was significant about Ypres?

In order to stop the Germans reaching the sea, the British needed to keep control of Ypres. Although the town was in a salient, surrounded on three sides, the Germans never captured the town.

> **DID YOU KNOW?**
>
> **Ypres is Belgian town positioned on a salient.**
> A salient is a 'bulge', or an area that sticks out into enemy territory.

FIRST BATTLE OF YPRES
The first of several important battles at Ypres

What happened at the First Battle of Ypres?
The Germans attacked the British positions to the east and north-east of Ypres *(p.83)*.

When was the First Battle of Ypres?
The First Battle of Ypres was between 12th October and 11th November, 1914.

How many British died in the first battle of Ypres?
50,000 British troops were lost in this battle.

Who won the First Battle of Ypres?
The Germans won the battle, although the British did hold on to Ypres *(p.83)*. This was important, as Ypres provided access to the ports to England, which meant that supplies could still be brought in.

> **DID YOU KNOW?**
> Although they held their position, the number of casualties at the first Battle of Ypres meant that the British Expeditionary Force was effectively destroyed as an army.

HILL 60
An important military position near Ypres

What happened at Hill 60?
During the First Battle of Ypres *(p.84)* in 1914, the Germans captured Hill 60, just south of the town. The British tunnelled under the hill and placed 5 mines under it, which blew up the German defences. The British then recaptured the hill.

When was Hill 60 attacked?
Hill 60 was captured by the Germans in December 1914, and the British took it back in April 1915.

Why was Hill 60 important?
Hill 60 gave the advantage of high ground in otherwise very flat terrain.

> **DID YOU KNOW?**
> Hill 60 was so-called because it was marked as being 60 metres above sea-level.

SECOND BATTLE OF YPRES
The first use of chlorine gas

What was the Second Battle of Ypres?
In the Second Battle of Ypres, the Germans attacked, moving two miles closer to the town.

When was the Second Battle of Ypres?
The Battle happened between 22nd April and 25th May, 1915.

How many BEF died in the Second Battle of Ypres?
59,000 British men died in the battle.

Why is the Second Battle of Ypres significant?
Gas *(p.93)* was used as a weapon *(p.89)* for the first time. In this instance the Germans used chlorine gas.

DID YOU KNOW?

The Second Battle of Ypres was the first major battle fought by Canadian troops in the First World War.

BATTLE OF THE SOMME
The 'Big Push'

What was the Battle of the Somme?
The Battle of the Somme was fought by British and French forces against the Germans. It was part of an offensive to force the Germans back and achieve victory on the Western Front.

When was the Battle of the Somme?
The battle took place from 1st July, 1916 to 18th November, 1916.

Where was the Battle of the Somme?
It took place on the River Somme in France, where the British and French armies met.

Why was the Somme Offensive launched?
It was part of an offensive to force the Germans back and achieve victory on the Western Front. It was also launched to help relieve pressure on the French, who were under attack at Verdun to the south.

What were the consequences of the Battle of the Somme?
The battle had 4 key outcomes;

- On the first day of the battle there were up to 57,000 British casualties compared with the Germans' 8,000. Haig continued the attack and, by November, casualties numbered 620,000 for the Allies and 450,000 for the Germans.

- At most, the Allies advanced by 15km along just part of the Western Front. The expected breakthrough never occurred.
- However, the Germans called off their attacks at Verdun, saving the French army there.
- The Allies developed new technology (the tank) and tactics (the creeping barrage), which contributed to victory later.

Why was the Battle of the Somme unsuccessful?

The battle is seen as an Allied failure for 3 main reasons:

- The Germans knew the attack was coming due to aerial reconnaissance. They moved away from the front line into strengthened trenches, some as deep as 12 metres.
- In the week before the attack, 1.73 million shells were fired at the German lines. However, they were not effective in destroying German dugouts or cutting the barbed wire. Additionally, over a third of those shells fired were 'duds' and failed to explode.
- Following the bombardment of shells, General Haig told soldiers to advance slowly towards the enemy trenches. He believed they would be undefended; but they were not, and heavy casualties occurred.

> **DID YOU KNOW?**
>
> Famously, there were 60,000 British casualties on 1st July 1916 - the first day of the Somme.

BATTLE OF ARRAS
An attack from underground

What happend at the Battle of Arras?
During the Battle of Arras, 24,000 British and Canadians attacked the German line from where they had gathered in tunnels. The British gained eight miles of ground.

When was the Battle of Arras?
The Battle of Arras occurred between April and May 1917.

How many British casualties were there at the Battle of Arras?
Over 160,000 British and Canadian troops were injured or died in the Battle of Arras.

Why is the Battle of Arras significant?
More than 2.5 miles of tunnels were dug beneath Arras, to allow the British to move and shelter from German attacks.

> **DID YOU KNOW?**
>
> **The tunnels at Arras included an underground Base Hospital.**
> It was the closest Base Hospital to enemy lines on the Western Front, and contained 700 beds.

THE BATTLE OF PASSCHENDAELE

'Perhaps the most hideous fight in the whole war' George Wrong.

What was the Battle of Passchendaele?
The Battle of Passchendaele was a joint British and Canadian offensive against the Germans, led by General Haig.

When was the Battle of Passchendaele?
The battle began in July 1917 and finished on 10th November 1917.

Where was the Battle of Passchendaele?
The battle took place in Passchendaele in the Ypres *(p.83)* Salient.

What were the aims of the Battle of Passchendaele?
Haig wanted to break through German lines and control the coast. He wanted to capture naval bases to make it harder for the Germans to carry out submarine attacks on British ships.

What were the results of the Battle of Passchendaele?
There were 3 key outcomes from the battle:
- After three months of fighting, Passchendaele was captured and Haig could claim victory.
- The battle came at a cost. A total of 240,000 British and 220,000 German soldiers were wounded or killed.
- In total, the Allies captured around 8km of territory, and Haig failed to achieve his main objective.

Why did the Battle of the Passchendaele fail?
There were 2 main reasons why the battle plan failed:
- As with the Somme *(p.85)*, the Germans were aware of the coming attack.
- Heavy rains turned the battlefield into a quagmire. Soldiers were knee-deep in liquid mud *(p.89)*, making it difficult to move.

DID YOU KNOW?

It was known as the 'Battle of Mud'.
With a few days of the battle starting, the area saw the heaviest rainfall since 1884! This completely changed the dynamics of the battle and meant that both sides were well and truly stuck in the mud!

BATTLE OF CAMBRAI
First large-scale use of tanks

What happened at Cambrai?
Tanks were used to move quickly across the barbed wire to attack the Germans. Big gains were made on the first night, but the Germans launched a counterattack and won back almost all of the territory.

When was the Battle of Cambrai?
The Battle of Cambrai was fought between 20th November and 4th December, 1917.

How many British casualties were there at the Battle of Cambrai?
There were 44,000 British casualties in the Battle of Cambrai.

Why is the Battle of Cambrai significant?
The Battle of Cambrai was the first battle that involved the large-scale use of tanks. Almost 500 were used.

> **DID YOU KNOW?**
> British tanks could be 'male' or 'female', depending on their design.

TRENCH SYSTEM
Terrible living and fighting conditions on the Western Front

What was the trench system?
Both sides dug networks of trenches to hold their positions on the Western Front. As they were developed they became more sophisticated, and became the soldiers' homes as well as where they fought.

What were the key features of the trench system?
The trenches had 7 key features.
- Frontline trench. This was the first line of defence, and soldiers attacked from here.
- Support trench. This had support troops, and was also a place to retreat to if the front line was attacked and over-run.
- Reserve trench. This was sited 100m behind the support trench. Troops could rest here when they were not on the front line.
- Dugouts. These were holes, dug into the sides of trenches, where men could sleep or take cover.
- Communication trenches. These were used to connect the other trenches together.
- Trenches were cut in a zigzag pattern to stop bullets travelling a long way down them during an attack, or to stop explosions from travelling along the whole trench.
- No man's land. This was the space between the front lines of each side's trenches.

> **DID YOU KNOW?**
> **Soldiers were rotated from the front-line, to the reserve trenches, to rest camps.**
> Typically, they would spend eight days in the front-line, four in the reserve trenches, and four in the rest camps or nearby towns.

NEW WEAPONS
New weapons mean new sorts of injury

What new injuries were caused by the new weapons in the First World War?
The rapid developments in military technology meant medical staff had to learn to treat new injuries caused by the new weaponry. These included shrapnel and large explosive wounds, head injuries, gas *(p.93)*, and shell shock *(p.90)*.

What sort of injuries were caused by First World War weapons?
The use of new weapons caused new types of injury in the First World War *(p.82)*.
- Bullets from rifles and machine guns, as well as sharp pieces of metal (shrapnel), could become deeply embedded in the body.
- Flying metal from explosive shells, called shrapnel, fired by heavy artillery, could cause large, tearing wounds.
- Bullets could break bones, which then stuck out through the skin. This was called a compound fracture.
- There was a huge increase in head injuries from explosions and bullets.
- Poison gas could cause respiratory problems, blindness, and burns.

> **DID YOU KNOW?**
>
> **In a study of 200,000 injured soldiers at a Casualty Clearing Station near Ypres, 58% suffered from shrapnel wounds.**
> 60% of these had wounds to the arms and legs.

MUD
Problems of hygiene and infection

What was the effect of mud on the Western Front?
Much of the Western Front lay on farmland, which became very muddy in rain. The mud also contained manure and fertilisers. Soldiers had to stand and live in wet, muddy conditions for long periods of time.

What problems did mud cause to medical staff in the First World War?
The mud caused 3 main problems for the medical staff:
- Trench foot *(p.91)* was a condition caused by prolonged exposure to the damp and cold. Soldiers' feet were frequently soaked and immersed in mud and water, and could not be dried. The skin rotted, which was incredibly painful, and sometimes led to amputation.
- Mud could enter soldiers' bodies and wounds along with bullets or shrapnel, causing infection.
- Explosives churned up the land. Many soldiers were drowned and lost in the deep churned mud.

> **DID YOU KNOW?**
>
> **The mud on the Western Front was more likely to cause infection because it was farmland.**
> Before the war, the use of fertilisers meant that there were more bacteria in the earth.

TRENCH ILLNESSES
Terrible living conditions cause ill-health

How did people get ill in the First World War trenches?

Living and fighting in the trenches caused soldiers to suffer from a number of illnesses, mainly just from the awful conditions in the trenches.

Why did the trenches make people ill?

The poor conditions, and persistent stress of living in the trenches, led to a number of physical and psychological illnesses.

What common illnesses during the First World War were caused by life in the trenches?

Life in the trenches caused many illnesses, but 5 of the most important were:

- ✅ Shell shock *(p.90)*.
- ✅ Trench foot *(p.91)*.
- ✅ Trench fever *(p.92)*.
- ✅ Dysentery *(p.92)*.
- ✅ Gangrene. *(p.93)*

> **DID YOU KNOW?**
>
> About 60% of soldiers are estimated to have suffered from trench fever at some stage during the war.

SHELL SHOCK
Breakdowns caused by the stress of war.

What was shell shock?

The stress of living and fighting in the trenches often caused psychological and mental health problems, known as 'shell shock'.

What were the symptoms of shell shock?
Shell shock could cause nightmares, loss of speech, uncontrollable shaking, and total mental breakdown.

What was the treatment for shell shock?
There was not much understanding about shell shock during the First World War *(p.82)*. It was often seen as hysteria, or an attempt to get out of the war.
- Some men who suffered from shell shock were accused of cowardice, and punished.
- Attitudes towards those who suffered from shell shock could be harsh, and they were often accused of cowardice and malingering.
- Electric shock treatments were sometimes used.
- Many shell shock patients were cared for at home or sent to mental asylums.
- 2,000 men were treated for shell shock, including the poets Siegfried Sassoon and Wilfred Owen, at Craiglockhart Hospital in Scotland.

> **DID YOU KNOW?**
>
> **Over the course of the First World War, 306 British troops were executed by the army.**
>
> They were found guilty of crimes such as desertion and cowardice. It is highly likely that some of them were suffering from shell shock.

TRENCH FOOT
Waterlogged feet become infected

What was trench foot?
Standing in cold, wet water led to a condition called trench foot, where the skin was soaked for such long periods of time that it began to rot. It was extremely painful and sometimes led to amputation of the foot.

How was trench foot prevented?
By 1915, the army understood that persistently cold, wet feet led to trench foot. Officials introduced several ways to try and prevent this.
- The feet were rubbed with whale oil to protect them.
- There were regular foot inspections by officers.
- Soldiers were instructed to change into clean, dry socks.

> **DID YOU KNOW?**
>
> Between 1914 and 1915, an estimated 20,000 British soldiers were treated for trench foot.

TRENCH FEVER
Flu-like symptoms, caused by lice

What was trench fever?
Trench fever affected up to half a million men, causing headaches, high temperatures, and flu-like symptoms.

What caused trench fever?
Rats and lice carried disease through the trenches.

How was trench fever prevented in the First World War?
By 1918, it was discovered that one way trench fever was spread was by lice; this led to the introduction of delousing stations.

> **DID YOU KNOW?**
> **Trench fever could cause temperatures of 40.5 degrees celsius, that lasted for five to six days.**
> Soldiers often sat around delousing each other to prevent this. The soldiers called this 'chatting', and it is where the word 'chat' originates.

DYSENTERY
Stomach pains and severe diarrhoea

What caused dysentery in the First World War?
Dysentery spread because of the unhygienic latrines and lack of clean water in the trenches. It caused stomach pains, high temperature, diarrhoea, and even death from dehydration.

How was dysentery prevented in the First World War?
The army began to purify water by adding chloride of lime, but many soldiers didn't like the taste.

> **DID YOU KNOW?**
> Latrines in the trenches were a common target for snipers.

GANGRENE

Infections that caused the body tissue to rot.

What caused gangrene in the First World War?

Gangrene is the death of body tissue, and occurs when blood supply cannot reach a wound, causing it to rot and produce a foul-smelling gas *(p.93)*. It usually affects extremities such as toes, fingers and limbs.

How did they treat gangrene in the First World War?

The only effective treatment for gangrene was amputation of the affected body part, to prevent it spreading and ultimately causing the patient's death.

> **DID YOU KNOW?**
>
> 'Gas gangrene' was common on the Western Front, probably because of the fertiliser present in the soil.
>
> It was so-called because the wound would produce a foul-smelling gas.

THE USE OF GAS

Chlorine, phosgene, mustard

What were the effects of poison gas in the First World War?

The use of different types of poison gas caused respiratory problems, blindness and chemical burns.

What types of gas were used in the First World War?

There were 3 main types of gas used for attacks in the First World War *(p.82)*.

- Chlorine, which caused death by suffocation.
- Phosgene, which led to death by suffocation but acted faster than chlorine.
- Mustard gas, which was odourless and caused more than 80% of gas injuries to British soldiers. It burned their skin, eyes and lungs. Mustard gas wasn't introduced until 1917.

What effect did gas masks have?

Soldiers were given gas masks, from July 1915, to prevent them inhaling gas, but sometimes they did not get them on quickly enough.

> **DID YOU KNOW?**
>
> Chlorine gas was described as having a smell like a mix of pepper and pineapple.

TREATMENTS
New methods for new injuries

What medical treatments did they use in the First World War?
Doctors developed new treatments for the illnesses and injuries that were caused by the fighting and by the conditions in the trenches.

What medical treatments for wounded limbs were developed during the First World War?
There were many injuries to arms and legs in the First World War *(p.82)* - 240,000 soldiers lost limbs through amputation. New techniques were developed as a result:
- The Thomas splint *(p.95)* was used to keep injured legs still, while soldiers were being transported from the front.
- Lighter and more mobile prosthetic limbs were developed for amputees.

Which medical treatments were used to treat gas injuries in the First World War?
Around 186,000 British soldiers on the Western Front were affected by gas *(p.93)* injuries, but only around 2.6% of them died. There were different treatments for different gas injuries:
- Soldiers affected by chlorine and phosgene gas *(p.93)* needed oxygen, and were kept in hospital for up to two months.
- Mobile shower units were set up for soldiers affected by mustard gas *(p.93)*, as they had to wash with soap and water to prevent burns. Their eyes also needed bathing as soon as possible.

Which medical treatments were used to fight infections in the First World War?
During the First World War *(p.82)*, doctors developed a number of ways to prevent wounds becoming infected in the dirty conditions of the Western Front:
- Soldiers were given anti-tetanus serum to protect against tetanus.
- Wounds were washed in carbolic *(p.54)* lotion, an antiseptic *(p.53)* solution. Once the wounds were closed, they were wrapped in bandages soaked in carbolic acid *(p.53)*.
- Amputations were carried out to prevent life-threatening infections spreading through the bodies of the injured.
- Wound excision, or debridement, involved cutting dead tissue away from a wound to prevent infection.
- The Carrel-Dakin method *(p.95)* was a system of tubes that ensured a constant supply of sterilised salt solution to a wound.

What new medical treatments were developed in the First World War?
Doctors developed several new medical techniques and practices to deal with injuries in the First World War *(p.82)*. These included:
- The use of mobile X-ray *(p.70)* machines.
- Blood transfusions and blood banks.
- Brain surgery *(p.102)*.
- Plastic surgery *(p.101)*.

DID YOU KNOW?

The introduction of the Thomas splint made a huge difference to survival rates of wounded soldiers.

Before it was introduced, soldiers with compound fractures caused by bullet wounds to the leg only had a 20% chance of survival. By 1918, however, they had an 82% chance of survival.

THOMAS SPLINT
A splint for broken limbs

What was the Thomas Splint?
The Thomas splint kept a wounded leg straight while the injured soldier was transported to a medical post. It reduced the death rate from compound fractures, from 80% to 18%.

CARREL-DAKIN METHOD
A method to help prevent infections in wounds

What was the Carrel-Dakin method?
The Carrel-Dakin method was a system of tubes that ensured a constant supply of sterilised salt solution to a wound, to prevent infection.

> **DID YOU KNOW?**
> This method is named after two scientists: Auguste (Alexis) Carrel and Henry Drysdale Dakin.

RAMC
The Royal Army Medical Corps

What was the Royal Army Medical Corps?
Doctors and medics in the army belonged to the Royal Army Medical Corps, or RAMC. They worked in different stations on the Western Front.

What was the chain of evacuation for the RAMC?
There was a 'chain *(p.69)* of evacuation' to get wounded soldiers to a safe treatment area. The links in the chain were:
- ☑ Regimental Aid Posts (RAP *(p.96)*).
- ☑ Dressing stations (ADS and MDS *(p.97)*).
- ☑ Casualty Clearing Stations (CCS *(p.97)*).
- ☑ Base hospitals.

> **DID YOU KNOW?**
> **The RAMC grew over the course of the war.**
> In 1914, there were 3,168 medical officers in the RAMC. By 1918 there were 13,061, and more than 50% of all Britain's doctors had joined the army.

REGIMENTAL AID POSTS
Closest to the front line

What were Regimental Aid Posts?
The Regimental Aid Post, (RAP), was the first port of call for an injured soldier.

Where were Regimental Aid Posts situated?
RAPs were usually situated around 200m behind the front line.

Who worked at the Regimental Aid Posts?
Each RAP was run by a regimental medical officer and stretcher bearers.

What treatment did a Regimental Aid Post give?
RAPs provided simple first aid for mild injuries, and sent soldiers with serious injuries further behind the lines.

Where might an injured soldier be sent after the Regimental Aid Post?
Soldiers with serious injuries would be sent from the Regimental Aid Post to the Advanced Dressing Station *(p.96)* or Main Dressing Station *(p.97)*.

> **DID YOU KNOW?**
>
> **There were usually four stretcher-bearers to a company.**
> However, where the terrain was especially rough and muddy, it might take six stretcher-bearers to move a wounded man.

ADVANCED DRESSING STATIONS
The medical post behind the Regimental Aid Post

What were Advanced Dressing Stations?
Advanced Dressing Stations were used for treating wounded soldiers that could not be dealt with by Regimental Aid Posts.

Where were Advanced Dressing Stations situated?
Advanced Dressing Stations were located around 400m behind the Regimental Aid Posts.

> **DID YOU KNOW?**
>
> **The Advanced Dressing Station was usually run by the Field Ambulance.**
> This was a mobile medical unit on the front-line.

MAIN DRESSING STATIONS
Well-staffed posts for injuries that went beyond first aid.

What were Main Dressing Stations?
Main Dressing Stations (MDS), were used to treat injuries that couldn't be dealt with near the front lines.

Where were Main Dressing Stations located?
Main Dressing Stations were located about 1,200m behind the Regimental Aid Posts.

Who worked at the Main Dressing Stations?
Main Dressing Stations had more staff than smaller posts:
- They were manned by ten medical officers.
- They also contained orderlies and, after 1915, sometimes nurses.

Where might an injured soldier be sent after the Main Dressing Station?
Severely wounded soldiers were sent from the Main Dressing Station to a Casualty Clearing Station (p.97).

> **DID YOU KNOW?**
> Main Dressing Stations were often located in abandoned buildings or underground dugouts.

CASUALTY CLEARING STATIONS
Larger medical posts

What were Casualty Clearing Stations?
Casualty Clearing Stations (CCS) were for treating more serious injuries suffered by soldiers.

Where were Casualty Clearing Stations in the First World War?
There were 2 main points about the location of Casualty Clearing Stations:
- They were normally a few miles behind the lines, to ensure the safety of the more seriously-wounded soldiers.
- They were often near railway lines, making it easier to transport (p.100) patients to base hospitals, or back home to Britain.

Where might an injured soldier be sent after the Casualty Clearing Station?
Patients who couldn't recover in Casualty Clearing Stations were either sent to a Base Hospital (p.98), or home to Britain.

> **DID YOU KNOW?**
>
> **Doctors developed a system of 'triage' at the Casualty Clearing Stations.**
> Patients were sorted into 'walking wounded', those who needed further hospital treatment, and 'moribund' cases, who had no chance of getting better.

BASE HOSPITALS
The largest and safest of the medical posts on the Western Front

What were Base Hospitals?
Base Hospitals were the largest and best equipped medical posts in the First World War *(p. 82)*.

Where were Base Hospitals?
Base Hospitals were mostly located near the northern coast of France, so that injured men could be shipped back to Britain.

What was the role of Base Hospitals?
There were 3 main roles that Base Hospitals carried out:
- They treated patients who required longer-term medical care.
- They grouped patients in wards according to their type of injury.
- Doctors assigned to each ward began to develop specialisms in certain types of injury and treatment.

What was the Base Hospital at Arras like?
There was an underground base hospital at Arras *(p. 86)*. It was opened in November 1916 and had waiting rooms, operating theatres, rest stations, room for 700 stretchers, and a mortuary. It had electricity and plumbed water.

> **DID YOU KNOW?**
>
> As the war continued, operations became more common at the Casualty Clearing Stations, as soldiers were often unlikely to survive the journey to Base Hospitals.

NURSING
Women on the Western Front

How did women get involved in nursing in ?
Thousands of women volunteered to become nurses - trained and untrained - during . Some were sent to France and Belgium to look after wounded soldiers.

What organisations could women join to become nurses in?

There were 3 key organisations that women could join to become nurses in:

- ☑ Voluntary Aid Detachments (VADs), were untrained nurses in.
- ☑ The Queen Alexandra Imperial Military Nursing Service (QAIMNS), consisted of trained nurses. QAIMNS was the largest group to work with the army during the War.
- ☑ The First Aid Nursing Yeomanry *(p.99)* (FANY) sent mobile units of volunteer nurses and first aid specialists to France.

> **DID YOU KNOW?**
>
> **Army commanders disliked the idea of women at the Front.**
> Many nursing detachments, such as FANY, had to fight for the right to work in a useful role on the Western Front.

FANY
First Aid Nursing Yeomanry

 What was the First Aid Nursing Yeomanry?

The First Aid Nursing Yeomanry (FANY) sent mobile units of volunteer nurses and first aid specialists to France.

 When was the First Aid Nursing Yeomanry founded?

It was founded in 1907.

 What did the First Aid Nursing Yeomanry do in the First World War?

In 1916, the British Army allowed FANY to drive ambulances, replacing the red cross drivers, and to give emergency first aid.

> **DID YOU KNOW?**
>
> The First Aid Nursing Yeomanry provided mobile shower units where the soldiers could wash.

VAD
Volunteer Nurses

 What were VADs?

Voluntary Aid Detachments (VADs), were untrained nurses in the First World War *(p.82)*. They were organised by the British Red Cross.

What was the role of the Voluntary Aid Detachments in the First World War?

The Voluntary Aid Detachments had 3 key roles in the First World War (p.82):

- ✓ They nursed in RAMC (p.95) hospitals.
- ✓ They were untrained volunteers, who often performed simple cleaning tasks.
- ✓ They drove ambulances.

> **DID YOU KNOW?**
>
> During the war, an estimated 38,000 VADs worked assistant nurses, ambulance drivers and cooks.

TRANSPORT
A system for moving the wounded

What was transport like for wounded soldiers in the First World War?

It was important to move casualties away from the front line as quickly as possible but due to the nature of the fighting new methods were developed during the war.

How were the injured transported in the First World War?

There were 5 main forms of transport used for moving casualties.

- ✓ Stretcher bearers carried injured soldiers away from the front line. This was dangerous and difficult work.
- ✓ Initially, horse drawn carriages were used to move casualties. These were uncomfortable and could make injuries worse.
- ✓ Motor ambulances could move casualties to clearing stations. However, they often got stuck in the mud (p.89).
- ✓ Once away from the front, casualties would be taken, by train or canal, to Base Hospitals on the coast.
- ✓ If necessary, casualties were placed on ships to be taken back to Britain.

Why was the transport of wounded soldiers from the battlefield difficult?

Removing casualties from the battlefield was difficult because roads had been destroyed, there were many shell holes, and the terrain was often very wet and muddy.

> **DID YOU KNOW?**
>
> Although canal journeys took longer, they were smoother and safer for wounded soldiers than the railways.

PLASTIC SURGERY
Finding solutions for facial injuries

What reasons were there for the development of plastic surgery in the First World War?
Some soldiers suffered horrific, disfiguring facial wounds. They often suffered psychological problems as a result of their appearance.

What treatment was available to disfigured soldiers at the start of WW1?
At the beginning of the war, the only solution was a mask made of tin.

Who was responsible for developing plastic surgery in the First World War?
Sir Harold Gillies *(p.101)*, an ear, nose and throat surgeon from New Zealand, pioneered several new techniques to improve the appearance of facial wounds.

What techniques did plastic surgeons use in the First World War?
The plastic surgeons of the First World War *(p.82)* developed a number of new techniques. These included:
- Pedicle tubes that were used to keep the blood flowing to skin grafts, to prevent the body from rejecting them.
- Bone and cartilage were used to make new facial features for soldiers who had suffered facial damage.

Where was plastic surgery developed in the First World War?
Queen's Hospital in Sidcup, Kent, was set up to care for soldiers with facial wounds. It was run by Sir Harold Gillies *(p.101)*.

How many soldiers underwent plastic surgery in the First World War?
By the end of the war, over 12,000 patients had undergone plastic surgery.

> **DID YOU KNOW?**
>
> About 16% of British soldiers who were discharged from the army had facial injuries.
> Of these, one-third of their injuries were classified as 'severe'.

HAROLD GILLIES
A pioneer of plastic surgery

Who was Harold Gillies?
Harold Gillies was an ear, nose and throat specialist from New Zealand, who developed plastic surgery *(p.101)*. He pioneered several new techniques to improve the appearance of facial injuries in the First World War *(p.82)*.

BRAIN SURGERY
New techniques for head injuries

What was the reason for the development of neurosurgery during the First World War?
The number of soldiers receiving brain injuries led to the development of neurosurgery thoughout the war.

What were the difficulties with neurosurgery during the First World War?
There were 2 main difficulties with neurosurgery in 1914:
- Head wounds affecting the brain were often fatal, because unconscious patients were difficult to move through the chain *(p.69)* of evacuation.
- Surgeons had little experience of neurosurgery.

Who developed neurosurgery during the First World War?
American neurosurgeon Harvey *(p.35)* Cushing *(p.102)* used new techniques to treat brain injuries.

How was neurosurgery used to treat brain injuries in the First World War?
Two main methods were developed to deal with brain injuries:
- Magnets were used to remove metal fragments from the brain.
- Local anaesthetic *(p.49)* was used because it reduced swelling to the brain. General anaesthetic was found to increase swelling and therefore made brain surgery more dangerous.

What were the results of Harvey Cushing's work on neurosurgery during the First World War?
Cushing's *(p.102)* techniques improved the survival rate from brain surgery, from an average of 50% to 71%.

How did the Brodie helmet reduce the need for neurosurgery in the First World War?
In 1915, the Brodie helmet was introduced to help prevent head injuries. It was made from steel and had a strap to keep it on the soldier's head. It is estimated that it reduced the fatality of head wounds by 80%.

> **DID YOU KNOW?**
>
> **Before Cushings' innovations, brain surgery didn't have a high survival rate.**
> However, by 1917 Cushing had increased the survival rate of his patients from 50% to 71%.

HARVEY CUSHING
Father of Neurosurgery

Who was Harvey Cushing?
Harvey *(p.35)* Cushing was an American neurosurgeon, who pioneered new brain surgery *(p.102)* techniques in the First World War *(p.82)*.

BLOOD TRANSFUSIONS
Developing the storage and transfusion of blood

What about blood transfusions in the First World War?
In the late 19th century, blood transfusions were given person-to-person and often resulted in infection and death. By the end of the First World War *(p.82)*, however, medical advances had made them much safer and more common.

What new techniques were used for blood transfusion in the First World War?
Techniques used in blood transfusions developed throughout the war.
- ☑ In 1915, Lawrence Bruce Robertson *(p.104)* developed a method of transferring blood using a syringe and a tube, as person-to-person transfusions weren't practical on the Western Front.
- ☑ Also in 1915, Richard Weil *(p.104)* discovered that blood which had sodium nitrate added to it could be stored for up to 2 days if refrigerated.
- ☑ Geoffrey Keynes created a portable blood transfusion *(p.62)* kit, so that transfusions could be carried out near the frontline.

How did blood banks help blood transfusions in the First World War?
By 1917, most casualty clearing stations used blood transfusions regularly. The building of depots for storing blood began before the Battle of Cambrai *(p.87)*. This helped blood transfusion *(p.62)* as there was an available store of blood to use.

How was infection prevented during blood transfusions in the First World War?
Before the war, many patients died from infections after blood transfusions. New discoveries prevented this happening:
- ☑ In 1900-1901, Austrian scientist Karl Landsteiner *(p.63)* discovered there were different blood types, which he named A, B, AB and O. This meant people were given the right blood, making transfusions safer.
- ☑ Aseptic surgery *(p.55)* practices prevented infection as a result of the transfusion process.

How did they prevent blood for transfusions from clotting in the First World War?
One problem with storing blood was that it clotted and became thick and sticky. During the First World War *(p.82)*, doctors needed to find ways to avoid this:
- ☑ In 1915, Richard Lewisohn *(p.104)* discovered that adding sodium citrate to blood prevented clotting for two days.
- ☑ In 1916, Francis Rous *(p.104)* and James Turner *(p.105)* extended the storage time of blood from 2 days to 4 weeks if it was refrigerated, by adding citrate glucose to stop it clotting.

DID YOU KNOW?

The blood group stored in the Cambrai blood bank was type O, which was safer to use with all blood groups.

LAWRENCE BRUCE ROBERTSON
Canadian Surgeon of WW1

Who was Lawrence Bruce Robertson?

Lawrence Bruce Robertson was a Canadian surgeon, who developed a method of transferring blood using a syringe and a tube.

RICHARD WEIL
American doctor in WWI

Who was Richard Weil?

Richard Weil was an American doctor. He discovered that blood could be kept fresh for up to 2 days, if it had sodium nitrate added to it and it was kept refridgerated.

RICHARD LEWISOHN
German-American surgeon

Who was Richard Lewisohn?

Richard Lewisohn was an American surgeon, who discovered that adding sodium citrate to blood prevented the blood from clotting for two days.

FRANCIS ROUS
American doctor who helped to develop blood banks

Who was Francis Rous?

Francis Rous was an American virologist. He worked with James Turner *(p.105)* to extend the storage time for blood, from 2 days to 4 weeks. They worked out that adding citrate glucose to the blood, and refrigerating it, would stop it from clotting.

JAMES TURNER

American doctor who helped to develop blood banks

Who was James Turner?

James Turner was an American doctor. He worked with Francis Rous *(p.104)* to extend the storage time for blood, from 2 days to 4 weeks. They worked out that adding citrate glucose to the blood, and refrigerating it, would stop it from clotting.

X-RAYS

Putting X-rays to work on the battlefield

Were X-rays used in the First World War?

X-rays were first invented in 1895, but they were put to more common use during the First World War *(p.82)*.

How were X-rays used in the First World War?

There were 2 main uses of X-rays in the First World War *(p.82)*:

- Before surgeons operated on patients with bullet and shrapnel injuries, two X-rays were taken of the wounds, so the surgeons knew exactly where the pieces were located.
- British Base Hospitals, and some Casualty Clearing Stations, had large X-ray *(p.70)* machines.

What were mobile X-ray units in the First World War?

There are 3 main things to note about mobile X-ray *(p.70)* machines:

- Pioneering radiologist, Marie Curie *(p.69)*, developed mobile X-ray *(p.70)* machines that could be transported in vans, and used at the Western Front.
- The RAMC *(p.95)* had six mobile X-ray *(p.70)* units on the Western Front.
- Mobile X-ray *(p.70)* units were set up in a tent at the back of a van, and powered by the van's engine.

What were the disadvantages of X-ray machines during the First World War?

The use of X-rays in the First World War *(p.82)* was problematic, particularly with the mobile units. There were 5 main problems.

- The radiation *(p.69)* from X-ray *(p.70)* machines could be harmful and cause burns.
- Pictures from mobile X-ray *(p.70)* machines were of poorer quality than those from the larger static machines. They were, however, usually good enough for the surgeons to work from.
- Soldiers had to remain still for a few minutes while the X-ray *(p.70)* was taken, even if they were in pain.
- The tubes of the X-ray *(p.70)* machine were fragile, and became too hot if the machine was used for more than an hour at a time.
- X-rays could only identify objects such as bullets and shrapnel. They could not identify fragments of clothing or soil in a wound.

DID YOU KNOW?

The original X-ray machines emitted 1,500 times as much radiation as they do today.

Get our free app at GCSEHistory.com

GLOSSARY

A

Abolish, Abolished - to stop something, or get rid of it.

Alchemy - the study of the properties of different matter and subsequent attempts to transform, create or combine them to make something else. Often used in relation to turning something into gold.

Amputate, Amputation - to surgically remove a limb from someone's body.

Anaesthetic - a drug used in surgery to remove pain by causing a temporary loss of sensation or awareness.

Anatomist - someone who studies and conducts research on the human body.

Anatomy - the study of how the body is made up internally, what it looks like, how it is structured and how the different parts are positioned.

Antibiotics - microbes that can kill germs that cause diseases.

Antiseptic - a substance that kills harmful bacteria to prevent infection.

Apothecaries, Apothecary - a non-medically trained person who concocted remedies from herbs.

Artillery - large guns used in warfare.

Aseptic - an absence of germs and harmful bacteria; surgically sterile.

Astrologists - one who studies astrology

Astrology - the study of the alignment of the planets and stars.

B

Bacteria, Bacterium - a microorganism that causes diseases.

Bacteriology - the study of bacteria.

Barber surgeon - someone who could cut and shave hair, and who also carried out basic surgery such as bloodletting.

Bile, Black bile - one of the four 'humours' in medieval medicine. A black substance observed in excrement and vomit, it probably constituted clotted blood.

Blood group - refers to the type of blood someone has and used to distinguish between different types for blood transfusions.

Blood transfusion - the process of giving a patient blood from a donor.

Bloodletting - the process of removing blood from the body, thought to be a way of preventing or curing certain illnesses and diseases.

Buboes - painful swellings in the neck, armpit and groin areas that were a symptom of bubonic plague.

C

Campaign - a political movement to get something changed; in military terms, it refers to a series of operations to achieve a goal.

Casualties - people who have been injured or killed, such as during a war, accident or catastrophe.

Catgut - a material made from the dried, twisted intestines of sheep or horses and used as a ligature.

Cesspit - a hole which has been dug to store sewage and waste.

Charter - a legal written grant, issued by a monarch or country's legislative power, permitting certain rights or privileges.

Chemotherapy - the treatment of disease through the use of chemical substances and drugs, most frequently associated with treating cancer.

Choler - pus or stomach acid found in vomit. It was one of the four 'humours' in medieval medicine.

Circulation, Circulatory - the movement of blood around the body pumped by the heart.

Civil servant - a person who works for the government, either at national or local level.

Claim - someone's assertion of their right to something - for example, a claim to the throne.

Conference - a formal meeting to discuss common issues of interest or concern.

Contagious - something that spreads from one person or organism to another, usually referring to illness or disease.

Council - an advisory or administrative body set up to manage the affairs of a place or organisation. The Council of the League of Nations contained the organisation's most powerful members.

Cowpox - a viral disease similar to but much milder than smallpox, transmitted from cows to humans.

Credit - the ability to borrow money, or use goods or services, on the understanding that it will be paid for later.

Creeping barrage - a slowly advancing artillery bombardment which attacking troops can follow for protection.

Culture - in a medical sense, a bacteria grown under controlled circumstances.

D

DNA - the common name for deoxyribonucleic acid, a molecule that contains genetic information and instructions about the development, function and growth of every organism.

Diagnose - to work out the nature or type of a disease, illness or medical condition by looking at the symptoms.

Diagnosis - the identification of a disease, illness or medical condition after considering the symptoms.

Dialysis - the process of cleaning a patient's blood in a machine, removing toxins and excess water, replacing the job of the kidneys.

Diphtheria - a serious bacterial infection that can lead to breathing difficulties, heart failure, paralysis and even death. It mainly affects children.

Dispute - a disagreement or argument; often used to describe

GLOSSARY

conflict between different countries.

Dissection - the careful and methodical cutting apart of a body or plant to inspect its structure.

Dud - a bomb, shell or mine that fails to explode.

E

Economy - a country, state or region's position in terms of production and consumption of goods and services, and the supply of money.

Epidemic - an outbreak of disease that spreads quickly and affects many individuals at the same time.

Eradicate, Eradication - to destroy something and completely wipe it out.

Extreme - furthest from the centre or any given point. If someone holds extreme views, they are not moderate and are considered radical.

F

Fasting - to deliberately refrain from eating, and often drinking, for a period of time.

Fatalities, Fatality - Deaths.

Flagellation - beating or whipping, often done to oneself to show sorrow for sins. In medieval England, it was an attempt to prevent disease.

Front - in war, the area where fighting is taking place.

G

Gangrene - the death of body tissue due to either lack of blood or serious bacterial infection.

General anaesthetic - a state of controlled unconsciousness using drugs, usually during surgery so the patient can not feel any pain or move.

Genome - the completed DNA set of a human, animal or plant.

Germ - microorganisms that can cause disease. The name was coined by Louis Pasteur as he saw them germinating.

H

Hierarchies, Hierarchy - the ranking of people according to authority, for example a colonel in the army being higher than a corporal.

Humanism - a philosophical idea that humans can make up their own minds and ways in the world, rather than being subject to the divine or supernatural.

Hygiene, Hygienic - a term for conditions or practices with the aim of maintaining good health and preventing disease, especially in regard to cleanliness.

I

IVF, In-vitro fertilisation - a method of helping women to become pregnant by fertilising an egg outside the body before returning it to the womb.

Immune, Immune system, Immunity - the body's defence against disease and infection, creating antibodies to fight germs and toxins.

Industrial - related to industry, manufacturing and/or production.

Industrialisation, Industrialise, Industrialised - the process of developing industry in a country or region where previously there was little or none.

Industry - the part of the economy concerned with turning raw materials into into manufactured goods, for example making furniture from wood.

Infection - the result of disease-causing microorganisms finding their way into a wound or suitable body tissue and multiplying.

Inoculation - the introduction of an antigenic substance or vaccine into the body to provide immunity to a specific disease. For example, puss from a smallpox patient was given to an uninfected person, giving them a less severe case of smallpox and future immunity.

Investor - someone who puts money into something with the expectation of future profit.

L

Laissez-faire - the idea a government should take a hands-off approach to matters such as public health or the free market; it translates from the French as 'let it be'.

Lance, Lanced, Lancing - to prick or cut open something, such as an abscess, and let it drain.

Lazar house, Leper's house, Leprosy house - a place to quarantine people suffering from leprosy.

Leprosy - a contagious and painful disease affecting the skin, mucous membranes and nerves; it can lead to permanent damage and even death.

Ligature - something used to tie or bind tightly; an example in medical use is around a limb to slow bleeding from a wound.

Limb - an arm or leg.

Local anaesthetic - a way to numb an isolated part of the body using medication, for example to prevent pain during minor surgery or stop an injury hurting.

M

Magic bullet - a chemical compound that will kill a specific germ without harming other cells.

Mass - an act of worship in the Catholic Church.

Medic - someone who has medical knowledge but is not a doctor.

Medieval era, Medieval times, Middle Ages - the period from circa 1250 to 1500.

Miasma, Miasma theory, Miasmata - the theory that diseases were caused by a bad air.

GLOSSARY

Microbe - a living organism that can only be seen through a microscope.

Mine - an explosive device usually hidden underground or underwater.

Minister - a senior member of government, usually responsible for a particular area such as education or finance.

Monasteries, Monastery - a religious building occupied by monks.

Monk - a member of a religious community, often living a simple life of poverty, chastity and work.

Morass - an area of swampy or very wet and muddy ground which is difficult to cross.

Mortality, Mortality rates - refers to death; the mortality rate shows how many people are dying in a society.

N

Neurosurgeon - a surgeon who specialises in neurosurgery.

Neurosurgery - the medical specialism concerned with the diagnosis and treatment of injuries to the brain, spinal cord and spinal column.

No man's land - the land between the opposing sides' trenches in the First World War.

O

Offensive - another way of saying an attack or campaign.

P

Peasant - a poor farmer.

Pharmaceutical - relating to medicinal drugs, the industry that manufactures them, and their preparation, use or sale.

Phlegm - the thick liquid produced by the mucous membranes, usually coughed or sneezed out during illness.

Physician - someone qualified to practise medicine, often used as another name for a doctor.

Physiology - the study of how the body works.

Pilgrimage - journey undertaken to a sacred place, usually for religious or spiritual reasons.

Pioneer - the first person to explore or settle in a new area.

Plague - a contagious disease that spreads rapidly.

Pomander - a ball or bag in which to carry pleasant perfumes so that bad smells (miasma) can be avoided.

Population - the number of people who live in a specified place.

Poverty - the state of being extremely poor.

Prevent, Preventative, Preventive - steps taken to stop something from happening.

Printing press - a machine that reproduces writing and images by using ink on paper, making many identical copies.

Production - a term used to describe how much of something is made, for example saying a factory has a high production rate.

Prosthetic, Prosthetic limb - an artificial body part.

Provision - the act of providing or supplying something for someone.

Psychological - referring to a person's mental or emotional state.

Purged, Purging - abrupt and often violent removal of a group of people from a place or organisation; medically, to make someone sick or induce diarrhoea as a treatment to rid them of illness.

Q

Quack - a name for a fake doctor or medical imposter.

Quack cures, Quack remedies - medical treatments that are unscientific so not expected to work.

Quagmire - an area of swampy or very wet and muddy ground which is difficult to cross.

Quarantine - a period of isolation where a person or animal who has or may have a communicable disease is kept away from others.

R

Radiotherapy - a treatment that uses radiation, generally to kill or control malignant cells such as cancer.

Raid - a quick surprise attack on the enemy.

Rational - when something is based on reason or logic, like science.

Reconnaissance - observation of an enemy in order to gain useful information such as its position, strategy or capabilities.

Reform, Reforming - change, usually in order to improve an institution or practice.

Regimen sanitatis - a set of instructions on how to maintain good health though a regime.

Repent, Repented, Repenting - to feel or express remorse and regret for one's wrongdoings or sins.

Rolling barrage - a slowly advancing artillery bombardment which attacking troops can follow for protection.

S

Salient - in military terms, a piece of land that protrudes into enemy territory; also known as a bulge.

Scrofula - a type of tuberculosis known as "the king's evil" in Europe at one time as it was believed to be cured by royal touch.

Sepsis, Septicaemia - life-threatening and potentially fatal blood poisoning, where an existing infection triggers a chain reaction throughout the body.

Shrapnel - small pieces of metal from exploding shells or bombs which caused injuries to soldiers.

Sin - in religion, an immoral act against God's laws.

GLOSSARY

Skin grafts - a surgical procedure that involves removing healthy skin from one part of the body and transplanting it to a different area.

Smallpox - a contagious and potentially fatal disease that causes a high fever, rashes and blisters.

Smog - thick fog caused by pollution, usually in cities.

Splint - a strong, straight device used to protect and support a broken limb, keeping it in place.

Spontaneous generation - the theory that rotting material, for example food and excrement, created disease.

State, States - an area of land or a territory ruled by one government.

Sterilisation, Sterilise - to clean something so it is free of bacteria; also refers to a medical procedure that prevents a person from being able to reproduce.

Strike - a refusal by employees to work as a form of protest, usually to bring about change in their working conditions. It puts pressure on their employer, who cannot run the business without workers.

Supernatural - an unscientific explanation for an event or manifestation unattributable to the laws of nature.

Superstition - a firm belief in the supernatural.

Symptom - an indication of something, such as a sign of a particular illness.

Syphilis - a bacterial infection usually transmitted through sexual contact.

T

Tactic - a strategy or method of achieving a goal.

Terrain - a stretch of land and usually used to refer to its physical features, eg mountainous, jungle etc.

Territories, Territory - an area of land under the control of a ruler/country.

Theory of transference, Transference - the theory that you could transfer a disease from a person to something or someone else. An example is the practice of strapping chickens to buboes during the Great Plague.

Tithing - used to denote a unit of land in Anglo-Saxon England that generally contained about ten families. It was also the name for groups of about ten men who were collectively responsible for law and order in their local communities.

Transfusion - the process of transferring donated blood to a patient.

V

Vaccination, Vaccine - from the Latin 'vacca', meaning cow. Originally it referred to giving a person cowpox to prevent smallpox, but is now used for all methods of introducing a weak strain of a disease as a way of building immunity.

W

Ward, Wards - A ward is someone who is taken under the protection and power of someone else, usually because it is believed that they do not have the capacity to know what is best for them.

Welfare - wellbeing; often refers to money and services given to the poorest people.

Workhouse - a place for poor people who were unable to work or support themselves.

Y

Yellow bile - pus or stomach acid found in vomit. It was one of the four 'humours' in medieval medicine.

INDEX

A
ADS - 96
Advanced Dressing Station - 96
Alternative Medicines - 74
Anaesthetics - 49
Antiseptics - 53
Apothecaries - 25
Arras, Battle of - 86
Aseptic Surgery - 55

B
Barber Surgeons - 26
Base Hospitals - 98
Battle of Passchendaele - 87
Battle of Ypres, First - 84
Battle of the Somme - 85
Bazalgette, Joseph - 61
Bevan, Aneurin - 80
Beveridge, William - 80
Black Death - 28
Blood Transfusions - 62
Blood Transfusions, WW1 - 103
Blundell, James - 49
Brain Surgery - 102

C
CCS - 97
Cambrai, Battle of - 87
Carbolic Acid - 53
Carrel-Dakin Method - 95
Casulty Clearing Station - 97
Causes of Disease, 19th Century - 40
Chadwick, Edwin - 57
Chain, Ernst - 69
Chloroform - 51
Cholera - 59
Cocaine - 53
Crick, Francis - 72
Curie, Marie - 69
Cushing, Harvey - 102

D
DNA - 71

Davy, Humphry - 50
Diphtheria - 76
Disease, 19th Century - 56
Doctors in Medieval Times - 24
Domagk, Gerhard - 66
Dysentery - 92

E
Ehrlich, Paul - 65
Ether - 51

F
FANY - 99
First Aid Nursing Yeomanry - 99
Fleming, Sir Alexander - 66
Florey, Howard - 68
Four Humours - 19
Franklin, Rosalind - 72

G
Galen, Claudius - 21
Gangrene - 93
Gas - 93
Gillies, Harold - 101
Great Plague - 38
Great Plague and Black Death Compared - 39
Great Stink - 60
Greener, Hannah - 52
Gutenberg, Johannes - 32

H
Harvey, William - 35
Hata, Sahachiro - 66
Hill 60 - 84
Hippocrates - 20
Hospitals, 18th Century - 45
Hospitals, Renaissance - 37
Human Genome Project - 71

I
Illness, WW1 trenches - 90
Industrial Britain and Disease - 56
Industrial Britain and Health - 55
Inoculation - 41

INDEX

J
Jenner, Edward - *42*

K
Koch, Robert - *45*

L
Laissez-faire - *40*
Landsteiner, Karl - *63*
Laughing Gas - *50*
Leprosy - *27*
Lewisohn, Richard - *104*
Lister, Joseph - *54*
Liston, Robert - *49*
Lung Cancer - *77*

M
MDS - *97*
Magic Bullet - *64*
Main Dressing Station - *97*
Medical Technology, new - *73*
Medieval Beliefs about Disease - *18*
Medieval Hospitals - *24*
Medieval Medicine - *29*
Medieval Treatments - *22*
Mud - *89*

N
National Health Service - *81*
New Medical Technology - *73*
Nightingale, Florence - *46*
Nitrous Oxide - *50*
Nurses, WW1 - *98*

P
Passchendaele, Battle of - *87*
Pasteur, Louis - *43*
Penicillin - *67*
Pest houses - *38*
Physicians in Medieval Times - *24*
Plastic surgery, WW1 - *101*
Polio - *77*
Prevention, 20th Century - *75*

Prevention, Renaissance - *33*
Prevention, medieval times - *23*
Printing Press - *31*
Protosil - *65*
Public Health Act 1848 - *58*
Public Health Act 1875 - *62*

R
RAMC - *95*
RAP - *96*
Radiation - *69*
Rational - *19*
Regimental Aid Post - *96*
Renaissance - *30*
Robertson, Lawrence Bruce - *104*
Roentgen, Wilhelm - *70*
Rous, Francis - *104*
Royal Army Medical Corps - *95*
Royal Society - *33*

S
Salk, Jonas - *77*
Sanitary Act - *58*
Shell shock - *90*
Simpson, James - *53*
Snow, John - *60*
Somme, Battle of - *85*
Supernatural - *18*
Surgery, 19th Century - *48*
Surgery, medieval times - *26*
Sydenham, Thomas - *36*

T
Thomas Splint - *95*
Transport - *100*
Treatment in the Renaissance - *32*
Treatment, WW1 - *94*
Trench fever - *92*
Trench foot - *91*
Trench system - *88*
Turner, James - *105*

V
VAD - *99*

INDEX

Vesalius, Andreas - *34*
Voluntary Aid Detachment - *99*
Von Behring, Emil - *76*

W

Watson, James - *72*
Weapons - *89*
Weil, Richard - *104*
Welfare State - *79*
Wilkins, Maurice - *73*
World War One - *82*

X

X-Rays - *70*
X-Rays, WWI - *105*

Y

Ypres - *83*
Ypres, First Battle of - *84*
Ypres, Second Battle of - *85*